HISTORY BY FOOD

RECIPES AND STORIES ABOUT THE FOOD AND FAMILIES OF OLDHAM COUNTY, KENTUCKY

Mrs. Nellie Miles Pollard at the Kentucky State Fair, stands in front of the Oldham County Agricultural Display that she helped create for a statewide counties' competition circa 1920s. (courtesy Marjorie Morgan Applegate)

Editors

Nancy Stearns Theiss, Jessica Jo Theiss,
and Ann Zimlich

Acknowledgements

Lucy Waters Clausen chaired the Cookbook Committee for
History by Food and helped steer the committee's direction
to collect the stories and recipes that appear in this volume.
Without her guidance, this would not have been possible
(and she provided some darn good food to help fortify the
committee's efforts!) Lucy has generously shared the family
histories of the Waters and Clausen families, including
the Waters and Henshaw histories which are integral to
Hermitage Farm. Betty White Leet and Judy Fischer also
gave a tremendous amount of time and energy to go "over
the top" in recording interviews, getting permission slips
and providing articles and photographs for the effort.
The other members of this very energetic volunteer
group included:

History By Food Cookbook Committee

Lucy Waters Clausen, Chairperson
Betty White Leet
Judy Fischer
Marilyn Geist
Janet Lopez
Teresa Crocco
Ellen Perkins

Harmony House Publishers
P. O. Box 90
Prospect, KY 40059
502-228-2010

©2006 by Oldham County Historical Society

ISBN-13: 978-156469-148-4
ISBN-10: 1-56469-148-9
Library of Congress Control Number: 2006937219

Design by RobinetteCreativ@aol.com
Cover photo: Boys eating watermelon (circa 1910, taken in LaGrange, Oldham County Historical Society Collection)

Printed in Canada

Thank You

A special thanks to Dot Carraco, history center
genealogist, who gave a last review of the
cookbook material.

The credit and names of all the folks and organizations
who have contributed to the stories and recipes are
listed in the index of this book. In addition the Oldham
County History center would like to express thanks to the
following for permission to use their copyrighted materials:

The Courier-Journal
The Oldham Era
Louisville Magazine

The Oldham County Historical Society operates the
Oldham County History Center which includes an archives,
genealogy library, hands-on museum and meeting facility.
The proceeds from the sale of this cookbook support the
efforts of the historical society which is a 501(c)3 non-
profit organization. The purpose of the Oldham County
Historical Society is to preserve, collect and convey the
history of Oldham County by telling the story of its people
and the events that shape its development using the objects
and artifacts that illustrate and symbolize that history.

Over 85 volunteers help with programs, collections,
exhibits and events for the history center. For the
Smithsonian Exhibit, Key Ingredients: America by Food,
the following volunteers helped to make the exhibit a
reality for our community:

Peggy Burge	Beverly McCombs
Bill Eisner	Helen McKinney
Alison Filippini	Evelyn Peterson
Bob Fortunato	Keli Quinn
Rhonda Hale	Rae Anne Roley

Introduction

In 2006, the Oldham County History Center hosted the Smithsonian traveling exhibit, Key Ingredients: America by Food. The exhibit is part of the Museums on Main Street partnership program of the Smithsonian Institute and state humanities councils. Through application to the Kentucky Humanities Council, the Oldham County Historical Society was one of the six organizations in Kentucky to host the Key Ingredients exhibit for 2006 and 2007. The exhibit was housed in the newly, remodeled 1880 Presbyterian Church Annex on the history center property.

This cookbook was developed as a part of the exhibit, to tell the story of Oldham County's history by exploring the food traditions and culture of our region. It was modeled after a cookbook that was developed by the West Chicago City Museum, Stirring Up History, that was published in 2003 after the Key Ingredients Exhibit had visited that location.

As Oldham County's landscape is quickly changing from a rural to suburban community, it was hoped that the stories and photographs would capture the flavor of its citizens, who have contributed to the local history through their family and work. As the community forges ahead in the future, the Oldham County Historical Society strives to affirm the importance of the individual and collective community memory to develop a more enlightened society that retains the identity of its past.

Robert Martin
President, Board of Directors

Kentucky Humanities Council, Inc.

Board of Directors
Oldham County Historical Society

Robert Martin, *President*
Raymond Simpson, *Vice President*
Kevin Eldridge, *Treasurer*
Sallie Haynes, *Secretary*
Harry L. Bell
Harry Bounnell
Lee Clore
Oren B. Clore
Denia Crosby

Howard Ferrell
David Gleason
Marian Klein Koehler
Sally Landes
Duane Murner
Shirley Orr
Tracey Leet
Stuart Ulferts

Smithsonian Institution

Foreword

This book is a compilation of stories that connect local food traditions to the families that have lived in Oldham County. These traditions are based upon recipes that are handed down among generations who immigrated to Oldham County and then adapted to the local natural conditions that favored a particular produce or livestock. Early immigrants of Oldham County consisted primarily of English, African American, German and Irish descent. Most people, until recently, grew their own produce and livestock, or at least, knew the neighbor who grew and produced it. Food culture is distinctive for every region based upon these local characteristics of culture and nature. In Oldham County, pork, mint, spring water, corn, wheat, eggs, apples, grapes, eggs, sorghum, squash, poultry, beef, diary products and beans seemed to be staples. Oldham County at one time, led the state in dairy production. Up until the mid 1960s, there were numerous slaughterhouses and food lockers where local meat was processed.

In our past food traditions, contact with the land was direct. Food traveled simply and locally from the land to the table. People ate what they knew. Families picked, canned, slaughtered, pickled, smoked and cooked their food together. As a result, stories were created from experiences and events. These experiences and events sensitize us to the community of people from our past who knew their landscape and their neighbor. The purpose of this book is to connect the people of Oldham County with the local community of the past so that the unique character of nature and culture are preserved, protected and cherished.

Nancy Theiss
Executive Director

Table of Contents

Oldham County's English Culture

After the Revolutionary War, pioneer scouts returned with glowing reports of fertile lands and beautiful waters open for settlement in areas like Kentucky. One of Oldham County's first English settlers was Captain Snowden, who after fighting against American troops, retired from the British military service and became a citizen of the New World. This story was written by a local historian, Lilburn D. MaGruder, who tells of Captain Snowden's discovery of Oldham County.

"Fear not ABRAM, for I am thy SHIELD, and exceeding great reward."—Gen. xv. 1

Shield Insignia from Amos Mount Civil War Letters: These letters are a part of a collection written by Amos Mount to his Aunt Amanda and Uncle James Mount. The Mounts resided in what is now the archives building of the Oldham County Historical Society. Amanda Railey Mount was the great niece of Elizabeth Railey Jefferson who was Thomas Jefferson's mother. (Oldham County Historical Society Mount Collection)

With an established government of Independence, Captain Snowden was moved to assemble a group of men to inspect Kentucky from the river side, with possibility of establishing a community composed of families who desired the better things in life.

With this purpose in mind, these men acquired a barge at Pittsburgh and proceeded to cruise down the Ohio River to inspect and explore Kentucky from the water front. It was agreed that an unanimous vote must be met to determine a location to stop.

Various stops were made, none to met agreement, this continued until the barge came to a bend in the river more curved than usual, there was revealed a sight these men had never seen the like. A body of water one mile wide, extending beyond eyesight in a perfectly straight line, moving majestically quiet, with no evidence of a current.

On one side the stony cliffs of Indiana, the other view brought thousands of acres of level fertile farming land. In the background, forests of many varieties of trees with size indicating uncountable years of growth.

In all directions, as far as eyes could register, this magnificent vision caused turning of the barge to shore, and there was found a small stream of water, emptying into the river, clear as crystal, and here the travelers found their first taste of real Kentucky limestone spring water.

All of this marvelous production by the Great Builder, so awed these men, they with one accord, bowed their heads and a prayer of thanksgiving, ending with a christening of name "Harmony Landing".

Some of the English families brought with them their slaves and inherited or purchased large tracts of land along the Hwy. 42 corridor. These farms or "plantations" raised crops such as tobacco, corn, wheat, produce and meat. These items were usually shipped via packet boats that traveled daily to Louisville. Other English descendants established businesses and smaller farms, and helped to spread the customs and traditions from their homeland such as Freemasonry. The first Freemasons lodge was established at Westport, Fortitude Lodge 47 on Sept. 1, 1818 and is the oldest organization in the county. These lodges were established with the settlements moving westward and were ordained and recognized by the Grand Lodge that was organized in England in the early 18th century. Freemasonry became very prominent in Oldham County during the 19th century when a Masonic university was established in Oldham County, Funk Seminary. One of the professors, Dr. Rob Morris, founded the women's organization, Order of the Eastern Star, which is associated with freemasonry. Dr. Morris was also recognized as the Poet Laureate of Freemasons during this time, one of only two people recognized with that title in the history of the Freemasonry organization.

In June 2006, the Oldham County History Center completed renovation of the 1880 Presbyterian Church building, the same church Rob Morris attended. The property for the church was deeded to the Presbyterians by the Mount family, who occupied the house which today is the Oldham County History Center Archives. In the fall of 2003, the history center acquired 33 letters written to the Mount family by their nephew, Amos Mount, while he served in the Union's 6th Regiment during the Civil War. These letters are now online at the Oldham County History Center's website: oldhamcountyhistoricalsociety.org

Rob Morris Pamphlet (Oldham County Historical Society Collection)

Hermitage Farm

Hermitage Farm was part of a land grant that was bought by Captain John Henshaw of Virginia in the early 1800s. He gave the land to his son Phillip Telfair Henshaw who married Sarah Ann Scott. They moved to Kentucky and began to build their home in 1832. They modeled their home after the Henshaw house in Virginia. During construction of Hermitage the Henshaws returned to Virginia to visit family when Phillip contracted scarlet fever and died. Sarah Ann Scott Henshaw returned to the Hermitage a widow with their three small children, Sarah Ann Elizabeth, John Scott and Lucy Mary Jane.

Sarah Ann Scott Henshaw lived at Hermitage until her death in 1862. Her daughter, Lucy Mary Jane, married Richard Waters in the mid-1800s and they too lived on the farm. During this time forty slaves lived on the farm including their weaver, Hannah, as well as George Page, who was central to many of the farm activities and successes therein. The Waters had five children and gave Hermitage to one of their sons, Phillip Edmund Waters, who married twice and raised 13 children on the farm. Phillip Edmund Waters is credited for bringing orchard grass to Kentucky, making Oldham County the leading orchard grass region in the nation. In 1936 the farm was sold to the Warner Jones family.

Under Warner and Harriet Jones, Hermitage became one of the most famous thoroughbred horse farms in the nation. Warner and Harriet raised their twin daughters at Hermitage. Warner Jones is the only person to breed winners of the Kentucky Derby (Dark Star), Kentucky Oaks (Nancy, Jr.) and a Breeders' Cup race

(Is It True). Additionally, in 1985, Jones broke the Keeneland yearling sales record with the sale of Seattle Dancer for 13.1 million dollars. In 1986 the Queen of England visited Hermitage after meeting the Jones through a mutual friend, Will Farrish in Versailles.

In 1994, after Jones's death, Carl Pollard became principal owner of Hermitage. Pollard and Jones became friends when Pollard leased two yearling fillies from Jones in 1970. They both served on the Churchill Downs Board of Directors and became golfing buddies. Carl Pollard and his wife, Bebe, have a son, daughter and stepson. Mr. and Mrs. Pollard still contribute to the thoroughbred horse industry and continue the tradition of Hermitage Farm.

Before grocery stores were convenient . . .

The following is taken from a letter written by Elizabeth "Aunt Betty" Henshaw on Feb. 18, 1884 at Hermitage Farm, of items that she is sending to her sister, Lucy Mary Jane Henshaw Waters, who has just moved with her husband, Richard Waters, to Locust Grove in Louisville. George, that Elizabeth is referring to, is George Page. John (who is mentioned to be sick in this letter) is Lucy and Richard's son.

Aunt Sallie Waters Ripley at Hermitage Farm, late 1800s (Oldham County Historical Society Water's Collection)

Oldham County's English Culture

Feb. 18, 1884

Sister Jane,

At last George has been after the fruit trees and has deposited them in the cellar for safe keeping and will be obliged to start from here when he goes tomorrow— so I will be sure to catch him—and I have gotten as many things ready to send by him, as I expect he can carry. All the eggs I sent are fresh laid—those in the old water bucket are the newest—have been laid since last Thursday. They are all packed in meal which will be good for use. I sent a box containing some of the large meat dishes that are "doing nothing" here and which I know you need. For you surely did not take anything with you and I know you have needed things to use for setting meat away in. I have at last "fished out" some of the crockery that I brought up here, among other things the plates . . . so I sent you eight of those that have been used regularly on the table; those that are left, together with what I brought up here, give me an ample supply until I know John will be glad to have one of these to eat out of for he says your new plates "won't hold as well as a saucer". I also sent six of those great big plates because they are so handy to use for so many purposes. You will see that I have reserved the whitest and best of them and sent you the refuse of the lot, and also white, I only sent you six. I kept a whole dozen. In the box that has the bagging around it I sent your cucumber catsup, at least, as much of it as was not utterly spoilt—and I filled up the empty space around the jar with some jars of preserves for you left nearly the whole stock of preserves here and you know we do not need them. In this box I put an egg (tied up in paper) which was quite a curiosity to me. I boiled it so that it might not daub up the jars if it was broken. Lest you should be bothering about the kegs boxes and so on that I send the things in. I will just say that I have no use for them—there is plenty of some sort left so don't send them back.

   I hope to hear that John has gotten well: I have been very anxious to hear how he got along with his small pox or whatever he had. I forgot to say, I put three beef tongue in the box with the dishes right on top along side of your black pitcher and your little bowls and tin pan. The barrel of hams I sent will do to use, Edmund says, as he probed them all but be sure to get rid of them before the skippers hatch out in them or they will get into your new meat. I started to smoke this meat today. I am having what meat bags have found, washed and will send them to you another time. Good night, and God be with you.

Your affectionate sister,
Elizabeth

Lucy Waters Gertsma was born on Hermitage in 1890. In 1906, her mother died and Lucy was in charge of the house and kitchen until her father re-married in 1910. Around 1920 she immigrated to Alberta, Canada with her brother, Phillip. There she met Owen Gertsma whom she married in 1924. These are recipes she always used. We believe she took them with her when she left Oldham County for Canada.

Hermitage Farm, home completed in 1832
(Oldham County Historical Society, Waters' Collection)

COFFEE CAKE
Submitted by Lucy Waters Clausen

- 1 cup melted shortening
- 2 cups brown sugar
- 1 cup strong coffee
- 4 cups flour
- 2 eggs
- 1 teaspoon cloves
- 1 rounded teaspoon cinnamon
- 1 scant teaspoon nutmeg
- 1 heaping teaspoon baking powder
- ½ cup nuts, some mixed dried fruit

Mix together and bake until springs back when you touch it.

RICE PUDDING WITH CHOCOLATE SAUCE
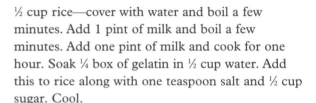

½ cup rice—cover with water and boil a few minutes. Add 1 pint of milk and boil a few minutes. Add one pint of milk and cook for one hour. Soak ¼ box of gelatin in ½ cup water. Add this to rice along with one teaspoon salt and ½ cup sugar. Cool.

Chocolate Sauce
Mix together 1 cup sugar with 1 cup boiling water. Stir in 1 teaspoon cornstarch, 4 big teaspoons vanilla, 4 tablespoons cocoa and a few grains of salt.

SCOTCH CAKE *(Cousin Phillip's Recipe)*

- 1 pound flour
- 1 pound sugar
- ¾ pound butter
- 3 eggs

Add to this mixture one teaspoon each of ginger, cinnamon and allspice. Roll thin (about ¼ inch and bake quick. (editor's note: put on ungreased cookie sheet, bake at 350 until lightly browned).

 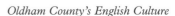

Elizabeth Waters was the sister of Lucy Grertsma. She grew up on Hermitage Farm during the early 20th Century and spent her later years living in LaGrange. She was called Bussie by her family members and always made wonderful bran muffins and dinner rolls. These rolls, however, were everyone's favorite. People bargained for the leftovers—if there were any. One of my children once ate a dozen at dinner.

Elizabeth Waters, was born (1906) and raised on Hermitage Farm (Courtesy of Lucy Waters Clausen)

ELIZABETH'S ROLLS

Submitted by Lucy Waters Clausen

1 yeast cake
½ cup lukewarm water
⅔ cup shortening
½ cup sugar
1 teaspoon salt
1 cup mashed potatoes
1 cup scalded milk
2 eggs
6–8 cups flour

Mash potatoes, add shortening, sugar, salt and eggs. Cream well. Dissolve yeast in lukewarm water, add to lukewarm milk, then add to the potato mixture. Add sifted flour to make a stiff dough. Toss onto a floured board and knead well. Put into a large bowl and let rise until double in bulk. Knead lightly. Rub over top with butter. Place in a casserole, cover tightly and place in refrigerator until ready to bake. About 1½ hours before baking time, pinch off dough, shape into rolls as desired. Cover and let rise until light. Bake at 400 F degrees until light. Yield: 2 dozen.

LUCY'S GREEN BEANS KENTUCKY STYLE

My Uncle George Waters moved out of state and married a wonderful woman from New York who was not accustomed to southern green beans. The only time Uncle George could eat green beans the way he liked them was when he came home to visit the family. He always asked my mother, Rachel, to fix greasy beans. This is not my mother's recipe but this is the way most of us and our families have cooked them for generations. I've never seen it written out.

Fresh or canned green beans
2 quarts for 6 people

country ham hock or ¼ cup jowl bacon, regular bacon or bacon grease drippings (2 tablespoons)

With fresh beans snap ends off and break into 2–4 pieces. Place beans in heavy pot with just enough water to cover. Bring to boil and add seasoning meat such as

Reduce heat to simmer and cook for 2–3 hours. Uncover and continue to simmer and reduce liquid. Beans on top will appear wrinkled and all will have darkened. With canned beans, drain them and then empty into pot.

THE HAMPTON FAMILY *Submitted by Margaret Ward Bromley*

My ancestors were among the earliest settlers in the Goshen area. Some in my family still own parts of the original property that has been in the family for generations. Former Judge, Julia Fields currently owns the property that was in the Shrader-Smith family since the early 1800's and Joe and Cornelia Nay still own land from the Shrader-Hampton ancestors.

My own grandmother, Anna Olivia Hampton, was raised in Goshen. She married D. Colin Ward and lived on farm-property that is now the St. Francis School. They later bought a house in LaGrange and helped farm land just over the Henry County border with their son, D. C. Ward Jr. and his wife.

Here are two recipes with details from the original cooks!

AUNT MARY'S FROZEN FRUIT SALAD

Mary Hampton was the wife of Al D. Hampton and was the mother of Oldham County resident, Robert Hampton and grandmother to Berry Hampton. She was a diminutive woman who always had a smile on her face and was a wonderful sister-in-law to Anna Hampton Ward. All the family loved this salad.

12 marshmallows
½ cup pineapple
1 banana
½ cup grapes, red or green
1 cup whipped cream

Cut marshmallows into bite-size pieces or use miniature ones and mix all the ingredients. Fold in the whipped cream and dressing. Put into an 8 x 8 inch pan and freeze until ready to eat. Place on a bed of lettuce.

Dressing:
Cook until thick:
3 tablespoons lemon juice or vinegar
3 tablespoons sugar
1 teaspoon flour

NANA'S CORN PUDDING

Anna Hampton (1890–1971) was born and raised in Goshen by her parents, Joseph Lawrence Hampton and Emma Smith Hampton who are buried in the family graveyard on the Hampton/Nay Farm on Hwy. 42. She lived most of her life in Oldham County. The corn pudding recipe is a favorite.

1 pint of corn (frozen, fresh or canned)
2 eggs beaten together
3 or 4 tablespoons sugar
1 tablespoon flour (only for frozen corn)
2 tablespoons butter
1 cup rich milk
    (include some half and half)
Salt and pepper to taste

Heat all the ingredients together, stirring until hot. Then pour into a greased baking dish and bake until done at 350F degrees approximately 20 minutes. Recipe can be doubled easily and makes a good custard base.

THE MOUNT FAMILY *Submitted by Gig and Craig Mount*

Mary Trigg Mount (1881–1959) and her husband John Mount lived on the Mount farm on US Hwy 42. After their son, John, married Letty Ware (1906–1998), they lived with the senior Mounts until they moved to Cardinal Ridge Farm, where John Jr. was the manager. On the farm there were dairies, cream separators, and chickens, so the cooks could use as many eggs and as much cream as they wanted. Craig Mount still remembers gathering eggs and getting cream from the cooler in the milk house for his grandmother Letty Mount so she could prepare the Charlotte Russe. For two generations, the Charlotte Russe was prepared for every Christmas dinner. In was served in a gorgeous old cut glass bowl.

CHARLOTTE RUSSE

1 quart milk
3 eggs
1½ cup sugar
2 envelopes gelatin
¼ cup cold water
1 quart cream
1 teaspoon vanilla
1 package lady fingers

Scald the milk and add the eggs beaten with sugar. Cook over hot water until thick or mixture coats a spoon. Add the gelatin that has been softened in the cold water. Remove from heat. Beat the cream with the vanilla until thick. Add half the whipped cream to the custard and pour over lady fingers (arrange the lady fingers in a pretty dish first). Cover with the rest with whipped cream and serve!

SARAH WARE'S ANGEL FOOD CAKE

This was Letty Mount's mother's recipe!

12 egg whites
1⅓ cup sugar; sifted once then measured
1 cup cake flour sifted then measured
   (sift six times)
1½ teaspoon cream of tartar
Pinch of salt
1 teaspoon vanilla
   (can be ½ vanilla, ½ almond extract)

Beat salt and egg whites until foamy. Sift in cream of tartar while foamy; whip until stiff but not dry. Sift sugar in gradually, add vanilla. Fold in flour, about ¼ cup at a time by hand. Put in an ungreased pan and bake at 325 degrees for 45 minutes—1 hour.

MRS. VEST'S PLAIN LAYER CAKE *Submitted by Joyce McKinney*

Mrs. Pearl Vest lived on Organ Creek Road for more than half a century. She did all the cooking on a wood-burning stove. During warm weather a summer kitchen was used. This photograph was taken prior to electric service at her home. Mrs. Vest is wearing the apron. Her white cake with caramel icing was a favorite.

Plain Layer Cake

1 cup butter
2 cups sugar
3 cups flour
3 teaspoons baking powder
4 eggs
1 cup milk
1 teaspoon vanilla
¼ teaspoon salt

Cream butter and sugar. Add eggs one at a time. Cream well. Add vanilla to milk. Sift dry ingredients and add alternately to mixture with milk. Pour into lined cake pans and bake at 375 F degrees for 35 to 40 minutes. When cool, frost with caramel icing. *(see Cora's caramel icing recipe in African American Culture)*

Mrs. Vest (apron on) with family at her home which had no electricity (Courtesy of Joyce McKinney).

COLE FAMILY *Submitted by Pat Cole Tipton*

My mother was Sadie Powell Cole who moved to LaGrange when she was a child. She married Bill Cole who also moved to LaGrange when he was little. Bessie Roberts had a walnut tree across the road from our home on Dawkins Road. Every year when the walnuts fell, all four of us kids had to go and pick up the walnuts—buckets of them—and then crack them and pick out the nuts so mom could make her walnut cake to give out to different friends at Christmas time. And she did the same with her jam cakes. The walnut tree is still there and producing nuts, but I'm not going to crack any more of them!

SADIE COLE'S WALNUT CAKE

½ cup shortening
1 teaspoon maple flavoring
2½ cups sifted all purpose flour
1 teaspoon soda
1 cup chopped black walnuts
1½ cups brown sugar, packed
2 eggs
1 teaspoon salt
1 cup buttermilk

Cream shortening, then gradually beat in sugar until light and fluffy. Beat in flavoring and eggs, one at a time. Resift flour with salt and soda. Blend into creamed mixture alternatively with the buttermilk. Stir in walnuts. Turn into greased and floured tube pan. Bake for one hour or until cake tests done. Let stand for 10 minutes then turn out onto wire rack to cool.

BROWN CASSADY FAMILY *Submitted by Nancy Cassady Doty*

In 1930, Mary Ella Brown married L. D. Cassady. At a bridal shower she was presented with a composition book filled with recipes from her friends. Mary Ella's mother, Nancy Brown, gave her the recipe for the So Good Salad Dressing and also for Long Time Pudding, which according to Mrs. Cassady, was the best pudding bar none.

LONG TIME PUDDING

- 1 can Eagle Brand condensed milk
- 1 cup whipping cream
- ⅓ cup raisins
- ⅓ cup dates (chopped)
- ⅓ cup pecans or walnuts (chopped)

Bake the condensed milk in a covered Pyrex pan for 4 hours at 300 degrees. Add whipping cream and nuts, raisins, and dates.

SO GOOD SALAD DRESSING

- 1 cup canola oil
- ½ cup vinegar
- ⅓ cup ketchup
- ¾ cup grated cheese
- 1 teaspoon mustard
- 1 teaspoon salt
- 1 teaspoon black pepper
- 1 medium onion chopped very fine
- ⅓ cup sugar

Put all ingredients together in a bowl and mix well until the sugar is completely dissolved. Put in a sealed jar and store in the refrigerator until you enjoy.

OMELET BELVEDERE

During the Great Depression, L. D. Cassady worked for a short time at the Emmart Meat Packing Company in Louisville. He brought home a cookbook called Let's Serve Something New!, *which normally meant something involving organ or brain meats. His daughter Nancy refused to eat scrambled eggs for dinner because she just knew it was really an Omelet Belvedere.*

- ½ cup cooked brains
- 2 tablespoons butter
- 3 tablespoons cream
- Salt and pepper
- 4 eggs
- 1 tablespoon butter

Dice the brains; melt the 2 tablespoons butter and add brains. Stir for a few minutes; then add cream and season to taste with salt and pepper. Keep the mixture hot while you beat the eggs, season them with salt and pepper, and melt 1 tablespoon butter in a skillet. Pour in the eggs and stir until they begin to set around the edge, then place brain stew in the center, roll quickly into oval shape, turn into hot dish, and pour any remaining sauce around it. Garnish with water cress. Serves 2.

HAYES FAMILY *Submitted by Judy Fischer*

As a small child in the 1950s I remember walking through the doorway of my Grandma Alma and Grandpa Melvin Hayes' little house on Sunday afternoons and being greeted by the delicious smell of chicken and dumplings simmering on the stove. It seemed that no matter how many people showed up, there was always enough to feed them. When Grandma was an old woman, I wrote to her and asked for her recipe. This is what she wrote back to me:

Grandpa Melvin and Grandma Alma Fields Hayes; baby is William Hayes (c) 1910 (courtesy of Judy Fischer)

GRANDMA ALMA'S CHICKEN & DUMPLINGS

"Take as much flour as you want dumplings, a scant teaspoon of salt, and a scant teaspoon of baking powder. Stir together and cut in a lump of lard the size of an egg. Add enough water to make a stiff dough. Roll out on a floured board and cut into squares. Drop into boiling salted broth and cook until done."

The following is how I make the dumplings since Grandma didn't give me complete instructions! I doubt she ever used a recipe book.

I simmer a chicken or two the day before, strain the broth and cool. The following day I discard most of the fat from the broth and add the deboned chicken along with some chopped onion, parsley and additional salt and pepper to taste. Sometimes I add a little garlic salt or powder. I then make the dumplings, using Crisco instead of lard, and knead them, adding flour as necessary to make them somewhat "tough." Grandma's dumplings did not fall apart! I've never been able to figure out a measurement of how much flour to how much shortening, but I've never had them fail. I divide the dough into the bubbling broth. They should cook slowly until they are done all the way through, which can take quite a while if you make thick dumplings. These are especially good leftover, as the flavor from the broth has a chance to really soak into the dumplings.

GRANDPA MELVIN'S EGG GRAVY

This is a recipe that my daddy, Ernie Hayes, would make for my three sisters and me on weekend mornings in the 1950s. We considered it a special treat. We didn't realize it was a family survival recipe from the Depression years. In the 1930s my dad's family lived at 15th and Ormsby in Louisville. On Sunday mornings the children would go to Mass, and my grandfather Melvin would fix Sunday breakfast while they were gone. When he'd see the children turn the corner coming home, he'd put the biscuits in the oven. They say he could make the best biscuits. Another thing Grandpa made to feed the children was leftover potatoes, cubed and diced, and put into bacon gravy. The Hayes family had lots of children and not much money to feed them. However, they always had enough to eat. During the Depression they lived on beans and recipes like this one. Grandma Alma and Grandpa Melvin could feed their large family with a little bacon grease, a few eggs, and damaged loaves of bread Grandma bought from the Bond Bread Company for a nickel or dime a bag.

Bacon Grease
Flour
2 to 3 eggs
Water or Milk

Pour beaten eggs into hot bacon grease in skillet (iron skillet is best, of course!) and stir and chop the eggs with a spatula until they are firm little pieces. Add flour to make paste and brown lightly. Add water and stir, adding more water if necessary to make a thick gravy. Milk can be used instead of water. Season with salt and lots of pepper and spoon over biscuits or toast. It looks just awful, but it's really good!

Oldham County's English Culture

Oldham County's German Culture

There were actually two different types of migrations of German cultures that came to Oldham County One migration was from German families that had settled in the Germana colonies before the United States was founded. These colonies were established in Virginia around the early 1700s by Germans who had indentured themselves for eight years to the Governor of Virginia in order to pay for their voyage to North America. As the westward expansion began, the descendants of some of these families moved into Oldham County in the late 1700s. The next wave of German immigrants began during the 19th Century when civil unrest in Germany caused many to leave their homeland in search of a more free and democratic life. The Nay and Clore families are examples of descendants from the Germana Colonies. Clausen, Stoess, Klein, Klingenfus, Hoops, Shields, Shrader, Klosterman, Dilly, Rieble, Varble, and Bottorff are examples of families that arrived in the mid-19th century. Many of the German families lived in the same vicinity, around Crestwood and Goshen and many raised vegetables crops, grapes for wine and smoked hams for markets, locally and regionally.

THE CLAUSEN FAMILY *Submitted by Elsie Roberts*

Three Clausen brothers lived in Magelson, Germany along with their sisters, Dorothea and Lucian. The first of the brothers to arrive in Oldham County was John who met and married Elizabeth Koenig and bought a farm off of Shiloh Lane in 1875. The second brother, Dietrich came after the Franco-Prussian War where he served as a Colonel and received the Iron Cross. The third brother, Hermann, came here at the insistence of his brothers and bought 132 acres of land around Skylight for $5,000 in 1885. It was told that he died of a broken heart at 51 years of age because he was very unhappy here. He knew nothing about farming and didn't like it! The sisters, Dorothea and Lucian, stayed in Germany.

Colonel Dietrich Clausen (Oldham County History Center Collection)

GRANDMOTHER LULA'S CREAM PIE *Submitted by Lucy Waters Clausen*

Grandmother Lula made this pie for as long as anyone can remember and it was perfect every time.

2 cups milk
⅔ cup sugar
⅓ cup flour
¼ teaspoon salt
3 eggs
1 teaspoon of vanilla
1 cooked pie crust

(This recipe can easily be adapted to make chocolate cream pie. Use 1 cup of sugar and 3 tablespoons of cocoa.)

Scald 1½ cup of milk. Mix together the flour and sugar and work into the remaining ½ cup of cold milk. Make sure sugar and flour are completely dissolved. Add flour mixture gradually to scalded milk, stirring constantly with a whisk until it thickens. Remove from heat, stir well, scraping sides and bottom. Beat egg yolks and add to pudding mixture, return to heat and cook back to a bubble and then cool it, covering with wax paper. Fold in vanilla when cooled and pour into pie crust.

AUNT MAMIE'S CORN PUDDING *Submitted by Harriet Clausen*

Aunt Mamie, Mrs. Nash Lindsey, was Mrs. R.C. Clausen's (Grandmother Lula) sister. After she married, she moved to Helena, Arkansas. During World War II, the women of the Helena, Arkansas Methodist Church, of which Aunt Mamie was a member, served this corn pudding to the soldiers. They loved it!

2 cups creamed corn (1 large can)

4 eggs separated—put the yolks in with the corn and beat. Beat the whites until stiff and fold in last.

3 cups milk, stirred into corn mixture

6 tablespoons sugar, stirred into corn mixture

1 cup saltine cracker crumbs, stir into corn mixture

Fold in the egg whites. Pour the pudding into a 9x13" well-greased pan. Bake at 350 degrees for 30 minutes, checking frequently once it begins to brown. Cover with foil and return to the oven. Cook until set; a table knife inserted in the middle should come out clean.

LULA ROSS CLAUSEN SHARES THESE STORIES AND RECIPES:

My dad, Elbert Christopher Ross, went to Louisville on a boat around 1890 to get work clothes. On arriving home he found this recipe in the box with his new shoes. He was surprised to find it and wondered who put it there and why. He was anxious for his wife, Julia Taliferro, to try it. She prepared the dish and they liked it very much and I know you will enjoy it too!

SHOEBOX CUSTARD APPLES

Quarter your apples, leaving some red peeling on. Put in a 2 quart casserole with one cup sugar and some butter. Bake until tender.

To fix custard:

¾ cup sugar

2 cups milk

3 beaten egg yolks (reserve whites for meringue)

5 tablespoons flour

½ teaspoon salt

Vanilla

Scald milk—mix sugar, flour and salt thoroughly. Add slowly to hot milk stirring constantly. Add beaten egg yolks and continue to stir. Cook until mixture coats spoon like cream. Add vanilla. Pour over apples. Cover with meringue and bake at 350 F Degrees until meringue is nice and brown.

"GRANDMOTHER AND RHUBARB" *Submitted by Lucy Waters Clausen*

My mother-in-law, Alvine Clausen, was a good cook but she never took much time to eat until the time came to eat dessert. She had a sweet tooth and rhubarb pie was one of her favorites. She often made it just for herself but was willing to share if someone came to visit. One day she offered some to my sons John and Richard. They took two bites and declared it tasted like "weed pie." They have refused rhubarb pie since then and I am sure they hurt their grandmother's feelings.

She sometimes made the pie using half rhubarb and half strawberries. I liked it better this way but she was a purest, and enjoyed her pie to be all rhubarb.

Alvine Clausen (courtesy of Lucy Waters Clausen)

ALVINE'S RHUBARB PIE

1 tablespoon butter
1 cup diced rhubarb
1 cup quartered strawberries
1¼ cup sugar
2 tablespoons cornstarch or flour
Pinch of salt

Pour into an unbaked pie crust and top with lattice, if desired. Bake at 350 degrees for approximately 45 minutes.

FRUIT SALAD   *Submitted by Harriet Clausen*

This yummy salad has been a favorite of the Clausen family for a long time. We always enjoy it over the holiday season.

5 eggs
5 tablespoons sugar
4–5 tablespoons of vinegar
    (The stronger it is, the less you will need)
Juice of 1–2 lemons
1/4 teaspoon salt

Cook the ingredients above in a sauce pan over medium-high heat until thick and then add:
    1 quart whipped cream
    1 lb. small marshmallows
    1 large can of pineapple
    1 lb. of grapes
    1 lb of chopped pecans or walnuts

SWEET CAKES *Submitted by Betty White Leet*

This recipe was brought to America from Germany
c. 1900 by the family of my late husband's grandmother,
Minnie Clausen Leet. Most people raised chickens and
gathered eggs to help feed their families. Usually, there
would be a chicken house for laying hens and sometimes
a part of the chicken house would be used for chickens
to roost at night. Often a chicken yard was fenced in to
keep the chickens safe. This picture, c. 1941, shows my
late husband, Kenneth Taylor Leet, with his grandmother
feeding the chickens and gathering eggs at the family
farm on Liberty Lane in Goshen. Perhaps they were
going to make sweet cakes.

*Kenneth Leet with Grandmother Minnie Clausen Leet feeding
the chickens, circa 1921 (courtesy of Betty White Leet).*

SWEET CAKES *Submitted by Betty White Leet*

1 lb. butter
1 lb. sugar
2 eggs
1 cup sour milk
1 teaspoon each of baking soda, baking
    powder, and vanilla
Flour enough to make a medium-soft dough

Cream butter and sugar until light in color. Beat
eggs and mix into batter. Stir in sour milk, baking
soda, baking powder, and vanilla; mix well. Add
flour enough for the dough to have a consistency
for rolling out, about 1 inch thick, and cut into
circles. Place cut out "cakes" on a cookie sheet and
bake at 375 degrees until lightly brown. Icing is
not needed. These cakes are not too sweet, they are
just right!

STOESS FAMILY RECIPES

Stoess family records indicate that the first Stoess immigrant, Charles J. E. Stoess arrived in the United States sometime during the turn of the 19th Century. He married Regina Dorothea Mang and they eventually settled in the Floydsburg/Crestwood area. One of the Stoess sons, John Samuel, started the funeral business in the 1882 and was continued by Milton Armstrong Stoess who also started a hardware business. Both these businesses are still in operation in Crestwood today.

Holly Fischer grew-up in Oldham County- her parents were Cleo and Add Stoess from Crestwood. She married Bill Fischer in 1957. Bill's mother was Jeanetta (Mrs. John L. Fischer). Jeanetta was a Buckner homemaker and loved to cook and got some of her cooking talent from her mother-in-law who is listed as Grandma Fischer in these recipes. Holly is a member of the Crossroad's Homemakers today. All of these recipes have a "German edge" to them- the cookies are particularly mindful of German pastries.

BILL'S FUDGE   *Submitted by Holly Stoess Fischer*

Bill first made this fudge in the 1940's.

2 cups granulated sugar
3 tablespoons of cocoa
⅛ teaspoon cream of tartar
⅔ cup milk
2 tablespoons butter or margarine
1 teaspoon vanilla
Pecans or Walnuts if desired

Mix and boil first four ingredients on medium heat until you can drop a bit in cool water and it will make a soft ball with your fingers. Cool a bit and add the butter, vanilla, and nuts (if desired). Stir well and put in a buttered pan to harden.

MOM STOESS' (CLEO STOESS) YEAST ROLLS

Submitted by Holly Stoess Fischer

Mom has made these ever since I can remember and I am 68!

2 ½ cups warm water
½ cup sugar
5 cups of sifted flour
3 beaten eggs
1 package or 2 teaspoons yeast
1 teaspoon salt
½ cup canola oil or butter
1 more cup of sifted flour

Stir yeast into warm water with the sugar and salt. Mix in one cup of flour. Pour in canola oil, stir, and then add the eggs. Add 1 more cup of flour, stir until smooth, cover and let rise.

REMEMBER: always stir yeast rolls over and under, not round and round. Knead the dough for 12 to 15 minutes, then roll out, and cut rolls. Put on tray and let rise and then bake in a 400 degree oven for 8–10 minutes.

MOM FISCHER'S COUNTRY HAM   *Submitted by Holly Stoess Fischer*

Country Ham
1 cup vinegar
½ gallon orange juice (optional)
Butcher's string
1 cup brown sugar
1 tablespoon cinnamon
1 tablespoon ground cloves
2 packages plain gelatin
1 can crushed pineapple

To prepare the ham, cover it with water and 1 cup of vinegar for 2 days (this helps take out some of the salt). Put soaked ham into a kettle of water and bring to a boil. After the water comes to a boil, turn the heat down and let the ham simmer for about 2 hours (I add ½ gallon of orange juice). The ham is done when you can poke a fork in and it comes out very easily. Remove from heat and pull out the bone. Pull the de-boned ham together and tie tightly with butcher's string. Mix together brown sugar, cinnamon, cloves, and gelatin and rub onto the ham. Bake ham in a 325 degree oven for about an hour then cover with the crushed pineapple and cook for another 30 minutes. This is easily the best ham I have ever had!

BATCHELOR BUTTONS   *Bill's Grandma Fischer's Recipe Submitted by Holly Stoess Fischer*

1 lb confectioner's sugar
5 eggs
½ cup butter
2 teaspoons baking powder
1 cup nuts
1 teaspoon vanilla
¼ teaspoon almond extract

Chopped almonds and citron (small amount of each, use your own judgment)
Enough flour to make a stiff dough, so you can drop from spoon onto cookie sheet.

Mix all ingredients and bake in a preheated 350 degree oven until edges are golden brown. Glaze with a mixture of lemon juice, confectioner's sugar, and a little water.

ALMOND COOKIES
Bill's Grandma Fischer's Recipe Submitted by Holly Stoess Fischer

2 lbs granulated sugar (4 cups)
½ lb butter (1 cup)
½ lb Almonds
8 eggs
½ lb coconut
1 teaspoon baking soda
Enough flour to make stiff enough dough
    to roll out

Beat eggs well, add other ingredients and beat to a blend. Roll out and cut. You can leave this out for a day before baking. You can ice with lemon juice, confectioner's sugar, and a little water if desired.

PEPPER NUTS *Bill's Grandma Fischer's Recipe Submitted by Holly Stoess Fischer*

12 eggs
¼ lb. Citron
3 lbs. flour
1 tablespoon pepper
½ lb. almonds
¼ of a lemon
2 teaspoons baking powder
3 teaspoons cinnamon
3 teaspoons ground cloves

Beat eggs well, and then beat in remaining ingredients. Take about 1 teaspoon of dough and roll into a ball with your hands. Leave these out over night. Cook at 350 degrees and cool. While still hot, shake in a bag of powdered sugar. Once completely cooled, store in an airtight container.

MRS. DIETRICH'S DUTCHMAN'S BRITCHES

Mrs. Dietrich brought these to homemakers for years and we all loved them!

4 eggs beaten well
2 tablespoons milk
Pinch of salt
Flour enough to make the dough stiff

Stir well, roll out paper thin, and cut with a circle cookie cutter. Pick up in the middle of the circle and drop dough into hot grease. Fry at 350 degrees, remove when golden brown, and sprinkle with powdered sugar.

ROCK COOKIES

Bill's Grandma Fischer's Recipe

1 cup butter
1½ cup granulated sugar
3 eggs beaten separately
2 teaspoons cloves
1 lb dates (chopped fine)
1 teaspoon baking soda dissolved
    in 2 tablespoons water
1½ cup nuts
3 cups flour

Mix and roll out, cut, put on greased cookie sheet and bake at 350 degree until edges are golden brown.

PECAN LOGS *Submitted by Holly Stoess Fischer*

1 teaspoon vanilla
1 box confectioner's sugar
1 14½ ounce bag of caramels
7 ounce jar of marshmallow crème
1 teaspoon almond extract
1 tablespoon water
Chopped fine pecans (to use for rolling candy)

Mix all ingredients together (except caramels). Shape into the size logs you prefer and freeze. Melt the caramels with 2 tablespoons of water (use double boiler over water). With kitchen tongs, dip the frozen logs in the caramel and roll in chopped fine pecans. Chill and enjoy.

SPINACH AND GRITS *Submitted by Betty Richardson Stoess*

This is from my mother's (Mrs. H.R. Richardson born 1902—now deceased) recipes. It is a family favorite. Can easily be made one day ahead; refrigerate and then bake the next day.

1 cup grits
1 stick butter or margarine
6 ounces of cheese (half cheddar,
    half American works best)
1 lb. spinach
2 eggs
½ cup of milk
½ package of onion soup

1 cup grits cooked in 4 cups boiling water. Add 1 stick of butter or margarine and 6 ounces of cheese. Cook spinach, drain well and chop, then add to grits, cheese, and butter mixture. Beat 2 eggs and add enough of the milk to make one cup liquid (pour remaining milk back into container). Add milk and egg mixture along with ½ package of onion soup into the grits and spinach mixture. Bake for 1 hour at 350 degrees in a greased Pyrex dish.

CHERRY DELIGHT

Submitted by Betty Richardson Stoess

My mother's recipe. Great and easy!

Crust:
1 lb. graham crackers
    (break and roll to crumbs)
¼ cup melted butter
¼ cup confectioner's sugar
Mix together and press into a 9"x13" greased Pyrex dish.

Filling:
1 8-ounce package of cream cheese
1 cup confectioner's sugar
1 package of dream whip
    (follow instructions on package)
Mix together cream cheese and sugar. Fold in dream whip and spread on crust.

Topping:
1 can of cherries (any canned fruit will work,
    but I prefer cherry)
Pour cherries on top of cream cheese mixture. Bake at 350 degrees for 8 minutes. Refrigerate when cool and serve chilled.

OATMEAL COOKIES

Submitted by Betty Richardson Stoess

This is another of my mother's recipes and we all still love it!

1 cup shortening
1 cup brown sugar
1 cup white sugar
2 eggs beaten well
1 teaspoon salt
1 teaspoon baking soda
3 cups of oats
1 teaspoon vanilla
1½ cup flour
½ cup walnuts or pecans
1 box of angle flake coconut

Cream together the shortening and the sugar, and then add the vanilla and eggs. Add sifted dry ingredients a little at a time. Bake on an ungreased cookie sheet at 350 degrees until brown.
Sometimes I will freeze the batter before I bake it; divide the batter in half, make long rolls and double wrap in wax paper and Reynolds wrap.

Oldham County's German Culture

MRS. DORA STOESS' 1952 JAM CAKE *Submitted by Betty Richardson Stoess*

This recipe is from Mrs. M .A. Stoess, mother to my husband.

½ cup shortening
1 cup sugar (½ brown, ½ white)
2 eggs
1⅔ cup flour
½ teaspoon baking soda
1 teaspoon baking powder
½ teaspoon salt
1 teaspoon cinnamon
½ teaspoon allspice

½ teaspoon cloves
½ teaspoon nutmeg
½ cup chopped walnuts or pecans
½ cup candied fruit
½ cup jam
¼ cup wine

Mix all ingredients together. Bake in a well greased mold for 30–45 minutes at 350 degrees. Shape of pan will vary the cooking time.

BEAUMONT CORN PUDDING *Submitted by Betty Richardson Stoess*

This recipe is from the Oldham County Homemakers Club cookbook from the 1950's or 1960's. We love it!

2 cups corn (I like frozen)
2 eggs
4 tablespoons flour
¾ teaspoon salt
2 cups milk
1½ tablespoon sugar
1 tablespoon melted butter or margarine

Mix dry ingredients. Beat eggs. Add milk to dry ingredients (no lumps) and then mix everything together. Pour into 9"x13" Pyrex and bake at 325 degrees for 1 hour. (I put 9"x13" or larger pan of water on lower shelf under the pudding or sometimes place the entire casserole in a water bath to bake).

CHOCOLATE CHIP OATMEAL COOKIES
Submitted by Kathy Widman

This recipe came from my husband's great-grandmother, who passed it on to his grandmother, who passed it on to his mother, who passed it on to me. His great grandmother was from Germany and lived until she was 101 years old. His grandmother also baked these cookies every year, until the last time she accidentally used salt instead of sugar.

1 cup sifted flour
1 teaspoon baking powder
½ teaspoon salt
1 teaspoon cinnamon
¼ teaspoon of nutmeg
¾ cup shortening or butter
1 cup packed brown sugar
2 eggs
⅓ cup milk

3 cups oats
2 cups chocolate chips

Mix all dry ingredients together. In a separate bowl put shortening, sugar, and eggs and after mixed well, add the flour and the spices. Add the oats gradually, then milk, and chocolate chips. Drop from a teaspoon onto greased cookie sheet. Bake for 15 minutes at 375 degrees.

RUTH DEIBEL'S PEACH PIE

My mother in law, Ruth Deibel, was a wonderful cook with many wonderful recipes. Another of my favorites was her peach pie. I baked this for my cousin who is an Arlington, Texas fireman and the cook in his firehouse. He liked it so much he made it for the firemen. One of the firemen took the recipe home to his wife. She thought it was so good she entered it in the Texas State Fair and won 2nd place! It is as follows:

1 unbaked pie shell
3–4 fresh peaches—hulled and cut in half
1 scant cup sugar
⅓ cup butter
⅓ cup flour
1 egg
¼ teaspoon vanilla

Put fresh peach halves in pie shell. Cream 1 scant cup sugar and butter. Mix in flour; then add the egg and vanilla. Spread the mixture over top of the peaches. Bake in slow oven at 325 degrees for about 1 hour.

RUTH'S ANISE COOKIES

My mother and father in law, Ruth and Ray Deibel, are both of German heritage. They have owned a farm in Oldham County for the past 50 years. D. W. Griffith was born on their farm. The stone work from his home was used to build the foundation for the house my in-laws lived in. They always had the family together to eat for every holiday. For Christmas we always had home cured ham, German potato salad, and lots of home made cookies. One thing Ruth always made for Dad was Anise Cookies. She died last year on April 5, 2005. Dad continues to bake these cookies and shares with the family. This recipe was in a cookbook made by the Fidelis Class, August 1948, of Bethel Evangelical and Reformed Church of St. Matthews, KY. It was put in by Ruth's aunt, Freda Lausman.

6 eggs
1 lb. confectioner's sugar
1 pound well sifted flour
1 teaspoon anise
½ teaspoon vanilla
½ teaspoon baking powder

Make sure you use a clean bowl with no grease on it. Beat eggs until light and add sugar. Stir one half hour. Yes, that is correct, 1 half hour. Add flour, anise, and vanilla. Drop with a spoon and bake at 325 degrees for 10–15 minutes. Make sure to use a high quality cookie sheet and grease and lightly flour it before dropping the cookies on it. Cookies are done when you can see bottom of cookies barely browning.

KIPFEL   *Submitted by Kitty Koenig*

½ lb butter (no substitutions)
2 cups flour
8 eggs separated
1⅛ cup sugar
2 cups ground English walnuts
1 teaspoon vanilla

Cut butter, flour and yolks together. Mix like cookie dough. Make walnut shape ball or a little smaller. Roll out thin and fill with 1 teaspoon of filling (recipe below). Bake on an ungreased cookie sheet at 350 degrees for 20 minutes. Top with sugar.

Filling: Beat egg whites, add sugar, nuts, and vanilla.

POTATO DUMPLINGS, NOODLES, OR MASHED POTATO SAUERBRATEN

Submitted by Phillip Koenig from his mother, Kitty Koenig's recipes

Roll Rump, Sirloin Tip, or Shoulder
1½ cup vinegar
1½ cup water
2 bay leaves crushed
10 whole cloves (no more)
5 whole pepper corns
1 tablespoon sugar
1 teaspoon salt
2 large onions, sliced thin
4 tablespoons oil
½ cup flour
Salt and pepper to taste

Mix water, vinegar, bay leaves, cloves, pepper corns, sugar, salt, and bring to a boil. Then pour hot mixture over onions and allow to cool. When cool, lay your meat in the marinade for three days. Turn meat once each day. After three days, remove meat and strain liquid and keep. Wipe meat dry with a paper towel. Then dredge with flour, salt, and pepper. Brown meat on all sides. When browned, add 1 cup liquid, cover, and place in 350 degree oven for 3–4 hours until tender. Serve on dumplings.

NUT STRUDEL   *Submitted by Kitty Koenig*

Filling

8 cups ground nuts
3 cups sugar
½ cup honey
2–3 cups milk
Cook together until thick

Dough

½ lb. melted butter
8 egg yolks
1 pint cream
2 cakes yeast
2 tablespoons sugar
1 teaspoon vanilla
6 cups flour

Heat cream then add sugar. Let cool to lukewarm and then add yeast. Let rise for 1 hour the first time. Work down the dough and let rise one hour more. Divide into 6 long rolls or 12 short rolls. Brush top with egg white and sprinkle with nut and sugar mix. (Do not beat egg whites). Bake 350 F degrees for 45 minutes.

Oldham County's African Americans

Most African Americans arrived in Oldham County as slaves brought from Virginia with families that inherited large tracts of land after the Revolutionary War. According to census records from 1860 in Oldham County, there were 6,217 white people listed and 2,431 slaves. The contributions of African Americans to the economy and culture of our community were very great. There were several famous slaves from this area, one being Henry Bibb. Mr. Bibb documented his experiences as a slave when he lived in Henry and Trimble Counties and his narratives were published and can be located on the internet. His wife, Malinda, was from Oldham County. He escaped to Canada and became the first black editor of a newspaper in that country. The history center has sponsored archaeological research on the Gatewood Plantation in Trimble County where Bibb was a slave before he escaped to freedom. Currently the history center is exploring the possibility of establishing a national heritage trail in his honor with the National Park Service.

Another famous citizen was Elijah Marrs. Mr. Marrs escaped slavery and recruited local slaves to enlist in the Union Army at Ft. Nelson during the Civil War. After the war, Mr. Marrs taught at two Freedman schools in LaGrange—there were only 17 in the state of Kentucky. He was a Sunday School teacher and at one time had over 142 children in his Sunday School class. He also was the first African American man elected President of the Republican Club of Oldham County in 1869 and first African American man to take the stump for the Republican Party in Oldham.

Last year, in 2005, the Oldham County History Center nominated a local citizen, Cora Harris, to the Kentucky Civil Rights Hall of Fame. Ms. Harris was a community leader in the 20th century and was the first African American to pass an entrance exam to attend a public school. She attended Central High School in Louisville by catching the train in LaGrange each day. Her brother, John, attended Lincoln Institute. Cora's father, Washington Bullitt, helped Elijah Marrs establish the Freedman school and Mr. Bullitt was one of the founding members of the AME Methodist Church in LaGrange. In later years, Cora was one of the first African American women to get her life insurance license to sell insurance in Kentucky—she worked for Mammoth Life Insurance Company.

The photograph depicts Cora with some of her friends in a group they called the "Crazy Eight Club" which started as a Christmas Savings Club. They met monthly and shared various dishes and friendship while also helping local efforts to support projects for the LaGrange Training School for African American Children. These are two recipes from Cora's file that she used for some of her gatherings.

Crazy Eight Club: 3rd from left Anna Goldsmith, Lizzie Crockett, Ann Reynolds, Hattie Harris, Flo Thomas Lewis, Emma Laura Johnson, Cora Harris and Mary Elzy (Oldham County History Center Collection)

CORA'S LIME AND COTTAGE CHEESE SALAD

Submitted by Nancy Theiss

1 pkg lime jello
½ cup hot water
1 small can crushed pineapple and juice
1 cup cottage cheese
½ cup mayonnaise
2 tablespoons horseradish.

Dissolve gelatin in hot water and add the rest of the ingredients. Pour in a greased mold or 8 x 8 pyrex dish.

CORA'S JAM CAKE

1 package spice cake mix
1 package instant chocolate pudding mix
½ cup salad oil
4 eggs
1 cup water
1½ cups blackberry jam with seeds
1 cup chopped nuts
½ teaspoon allspice

Grease and flour 3 round cake pans (line bottoms with wax paper). Mix all the ingredients together and bake at 350F degrees until cake is firm to touch.

Caramel Icing for Cake
Melt ½ cup butter and add 2 cups of brown sugar. Boil together for 2 minutes then add ¼ cup milk and keep stirring until the mixture boils again. Let this cool completely.

Add to the cooled mixture 1¾ to 2 cups of confectioner's sugar until spreading consistency.

AUNT GEORGE ANN'S FRUIT CAKE *Submitted by Margaret Bromley*

Aunt George Ann was a freed African American slave woman who lived at the Albert Ballard Smith home until her death. She is buried in the family cemetery. The Smith home and farm is across from the Goshen Store and is currently owned by a descendent of the family, Julia Fields. Although fruit cake is not everyone's favorite, this one is delicious. When baked, it is dark in color. Notice that the recipe is often measured in pounds.

¾ lb butter
½ lb currants
1 cup jam
1¼ cup sugar
½ cup molasses
2 cups sifted flour
5 eggs
½ cup cream
¼ to ½ cup whiskey
1 lb candied fruit
1 cup nuts
½ teaspoon soda
½ teaspoon nutmeg
1 tablespoon cinnamon
1 teaspoon all spice

Mix fruit, raisins, currants and nuts in bowl and sprinkle with a little flour. Cream the sugar and butter then add jam and molasses. Add flour and cream; alternating until both are blended in the mixture and then add the eggs. Blend in the fruit, nuts and finally the whiskey. Cover and let sit overnight. Bake the next day; if batter is too stiff, add a little milk or whiskey. Place a pan of water in the bottom of the oven and bake slowly on the middle rack for 2 hours at 300 degrees in a greased and floured pan lined with brown paper.

Emma Laura Johnson's Salt Rising Bread and Burnt Sugar Cake *Submitted by Emma Laura Johnson*

I was born in 1913 on Jericho Road in LaGrange. When I was six I began watching my grandmother, Emma Ross, prepare and bake salt rising bread and this is her recipe. Following the Salt Rising Bread recipe is a family recipe for Burnt Sugar Cake.

Emma Laura Johnson served as pianist for the First Street Baptist Church and Pleasant View Baptist Church for over 50 years (Oldham County Center Collection)

SALT RISING BREAD

1 cup milk
1 tablespoon sugar
½ cup cornmeal
1 teaspoon salt

2 cups flour
3 tablespoons sugar
2 cups + 3 tablespoons warm water
3 tablespoons melted fat

Scald the milk. With a wooden spoon stir in sugar, cornmeal and salt. Pour into a jar and set in hot sun for 10–12 hours

Add these ingredients and beat until sponge-like. Set back in sun until batter is light and full of bubbles. Add 8 cups of flour to make a stiff dough. Place dough in greased pan and allow to double in size. Bake for 15 minutes at 350 degree then increase heat to 425 for 45 minutes until done.

BURNT SUGAR CAKE

1½ cups sugar
½ cup burnt sugar liquid (see below)
3 eggs
⅔ cup butter
¼ teaspoon salt
3 cups cake flour
3 teaspoons baking powder
1 cup cold water
1 teaspoon vanilla

Cream butter and sugar slowly. Add ½ cup burnt sugar liquid. Mix in well beaten eggs. Add baking powder and flour alternating with water. Add vanilla. Bake at 350 degrees until fork ready. Top with caramel icing

Make burnt sugar by melting 1 cup sugar in aluminum pan on hot fire. When sugar turns dark brown, add 1 cup boiling water and boil hard for 5 minutes.

KRISTINE'S KOOL AID ICE CREAM

Submitted by Emma Jane Johnson Walls

My parents, Christine and Leavie Johnson moved our family from downtown LaGrange out to my grandparent's farm, Lizzie and Gipson Thompson, on Jericho Road. We moved there in 1937, the year of the great flood, when I was five years old along with my younger siblings, Dorothy Jewell and Leon Johnson.

High School Students in Domestic Science class at Lincoln Institute circa 1915 (Oldham County Historical Society Collection)

Life on the farm was interesting and educational. While measuring to build wagons and farm tools, my grandfather taught me fractions. There were lots of chores on the farm; feeding the animals, planting and cultivating crops, chopping firewood, carrying water from the spring and gathering eggs from the hen house . . . but it taught us responsibility. There was also many fun things to do such as picking wild berries, gathering nuts, wading in the creek, climbing trees, fishing and riding in the horse and buggy with our grandparents.

We attended elementary school in downtown LaGrange up to grade 10. Riding the school bus was a challenge. Because of segregation, we would pass other schools en route to the Lincoln Institute in Simpsonville, to complete high school. We lived at the beginning of the bus line which required us to board the bus at 6am and not return home most days till 6pm. Thus summer vacations were always welcome. Summertime meant softball games, county fairs, carnivals, church functions and circuses. Lots of the children in our neighborhood were relatives, so playmates were plentiful.

Many Sunday afternoons mother would make our favorite Kool-Aid ice cream. It allows for a choice of flavors, is inexpensive to make and you can even add fresh seasonal fruit. I've made it many times for my four children and they love it. Our favorite is Orange Kool-Aid with crushed pineapple added half-way through the freezing.

After 52 years as an RN, being one of the first Black RN's at Clark Memorial Hospital, raising 4 lovely children and having a great husband who was a head chef, I still regard my life in LaGrange as a very valuable experience.

CHRISTINE'S KOOL-AID ICE CREAM

1 package Kool-Aid (any flavor)
1 3 oz package Jell-O (same flavor)
1 can Eagle Brand condensed milk
1 quart 2% or whole milk
2 pints heavy cream
1½ cups sugar
2 cups water for Kool-Aid
1½ cups hot water for Jell-O

Mix Kool-Aid with 1½ cups sugar and 2 cups water in a large bowl. Mix Jell-O and 1½ cups hot water, stirring well until dissolved. Combine Jell-O and Kool-Aid in large bowl. Add condensed milk slowly and stir well. Add heavy cream and stir well.

Add 2 cups milk and stir. Taste for sweetness and gradually add more sugar if needed. Pour into freezer canister leaving 1 inch space from the top. Freeze according to your ice cream freezer instructions.

I start the canister turning before filling with ice, this helps it turn easily. Wait until contents are getting mushy before adding mashed fruit. The motor will start to sound like it's pulling hard. Open freezer to avoid salt from entering, stirring quickly. Replace dasher and lid and continue freezing until firm.

DIANE BOOKER'S FRIED CHICKEN   *Submitted by Diane Booker*

Seems like everyone asks for Diane Booker's fried chicken, at weddings, funerals, and family occasions. The secret is to cut up your chicken and then let it soak in salt water for ½ day in the refrigerator. Drain it, roll it in a flour mixture of:

4 cups plain flour
2 tablespoons of Lawry's Seasoned Salt
1 tablespoon of black pepper
½ tablespoons of garlic powder
1 teaspoon of regular salt

Deep fry in Crisco shortening, not oil, because shortening browns better than oil. Deep fry covered in iron skillet, till golden brown about 30 minutes, turning every 12 minutes. Drain on paper towels.

IRISH CULTURE

Irish families came to Oldham County with the advent of the railroad. Many Irish worked for the railroad companies and it was during this time, the 1850s, that the first Catholic Church was organized in the county in LaGrange. Priests from the Cathedral of the Assumption and St. Joseph's Church in Louisville served the Catholics of Oldham County. In 1871 a resident pastor was appointed for St. Aloysius Church in Pewee Valley, and LaGrange Catholics formed its Mission Church.

Mary Immaculate Church in LaGrange was dedicated on Dec. 6, 1875 on what is now Madison Street between 1st and 2nd Avenues. The list of pewholders: Alex McKie, Mr. A. Carrol, Pat O'Donnell, Joseph Sauer, Ned Kenney, Michael Kenney, Mrs. L. A. Conners, James McLaughlin, Thomas Curley, Dan Delaney, Maureice Whelan, John Donaghue and George Boemicke.

When we think of Irish we often think of good stews. The following are some recipes for good Irish stew that were submitted by several folks of Irish descent:

KALE GARLIC STEW *Submitted by Joyce Keibler*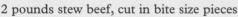

3 tablespoons olive oil
½ pound smoked sausage
1 large diced onion
6-8 cloves garlic, crushed
4 large diced potatoes
1 large bunch kale
    (washed, sliced and slivered)
2 quarts water or chicken broth
2 16-ounce cans white beans
Lots of pepper
Salt to taste

Heat oil in large pot. Add meat, browning and breaking into small pieces. Add diced onion and garlic; cook till soft. Add diced potatoes and kale with broth and water to pot. Bring to a boil, then simmer 25 minutes. Mash mixture with a fork, add beans and heat.

OVEN BEEF STEW *Submitted by Jeanne Gibson*

2 pounds stew beef, cut in bite size pieces
1 medium sliced onion
1 stalk of celery, cut diagonally
6 carrots, cut into chunks
2 teaspoons salt
1 tablespoon sugar
1 tablespoon tapioca pudding
½ cup tomato juice or V-8 juice

Put meat and vegetables in 7 x 11 pan. Sprinkle dry ingredients over meat, pour juice over all and cover with foil. Bake at 250 F degrees for 4 hours.

Ruth Melone Klingenfus shares some Irish food memories from her family

When I was a young girl in the 1930s, my grandparents had a three gallon ice cream freezer. Making ice cream was a special occasion then, like at a family get-together or an ice cream supper at church, since getting ice was a problem. A few people had their own ice houses on their farms. They would get ice off the pond in winter by cutting it with a big heavy knife and pulling it out with the help of a horse. They would load it onto the wagon and store it underground in the ice house with straw or sawdust in between, so it wouldn't melt as easily as the weather warmed. There was an ice house in Pewee Valley from the early 1900s until the 1930s where the streetcar line was. They'd bring the ice out from Louisville in big 100

Ice House on Ruth Melone Klingenfus and Carl Klingenfus Farm in Crestwood (courtesy of Ruth Melone Klingenfus)

pound blocks. A man by the name of William Hampton delivered ice to people's houses in Crestwood in the 1920s in his wagon. People put a little sign in their windows turned to "50" or whatever quantity you wanted. He would chip off a piece of ice and bring it in and put it in your ice box. In the 1930s we got electricity and no longer needed the ice man.

In the summertime when my children lived at home on our dairy farm in Crestwood, we would make ice cream almost every day from the cream our own cows provided. The youngest kids turned the crank first, because it got harder to turn as the cream mixture cooled. Then it would be the older ones' turn. When the ice cream was ready, everyone wanted to lick the dasher!

Here are some ice cream recipes from Ruth and from other contributors:

Ruth's Ice Cream Sherbet

1 can crushed pineapple
1 small can orange juice undiluted
1 small can frozen lemonade undiluted
1 sliced bananas

Add all the above together. Add milk to the line on the ice cream churn then work the ice cream freezer. We had a 1½ gallon freezer.

Oreo Ice Cream Dessert *Submitted by Mary Beth Westbrook*

My mom and my sister, Janet Pate, brought this recipe to our family. It was a favorite during the holiday season when my mom hosted her pinochle club. She started the pinochle club in Westport, Kentucky with Clarice Chambers and Genevieve Winters. I make this recipe every year for my daughter, Natalie's birthday. It is her favorite.

25 Oreo Sandwich cookies crushed
½ cup butter or margarine

Melt margarine and mix with crushed cookies. Press into a 9 x 13 greased pan. Freeze for 30 minutes.

Mix together ½ gallon vanilla ice cream with 9 ounces of crushed peppermint candies. Place on top of cookie crust and put in freezer.

Mix together on the stove:
  ½ cup margarine or butter
  ⅔ cup chocolate chips
  2 cups powdered sugar
  10 ounces evaporated milk

Boil for 8 minutes until thick. Allow to cool and pour on top of ice cream. Freeze and decorate.

Other Cultures in Oldham County

Hispanic Culture

The Hispanic culture has earned a prominent place in both the economy and culture of Oldham County. Many Hispanic families have settled here and their children are now first generation citizens. Leno and Martina Gonzalez became U.S. citizens and settled in Oldham County almost 20 years ago raising their three sons, Aaron, David and Joshua here. Martina and Leno were raised in Taretan in Michoachan, Mexico. This area of Mexico borders the Pacific Ocean and is famous for the migration of millions of monarch butterflies that spend the winter there. This region is very tropical and warm, with the lower temperatures during winter averaging 65 F degrees.

The Gonzalez family makes return pilgrimages to their homeland to visit family and friends. The boys, although thoroughly Americanized, participate in the traditions, customs and holidays when they visit Mexico. These celebrations include Saint Patrons Day, Cinco de Mayo, Days of Wiseman, Guadalupe Day, birthdays, and El Día de los Muertos or All Souls' Day.

It is traditional in Mexico for people to visit their family graves on November 2, Día de los Muertos or All Souls' Day as a mark of love and respect. They take with them a special round sweet bread that has a faint taste of licorice, el Pan del Muerto (Bread of the Dead), that is decorated with a cross made of baked dough in the form of a skeleton's head. Street vendors sell candy skulls and write your name on them with icing. These visits are not full of sorrow but rather a celebration like a picnic in which the dead are symbolically participating. Everything is festive and brilliant, colorful flowers and clothes are worn by members of family parties that are tending the graves in the family plots. During the evening, candles are lit at each graveside making a luminary of sparkling lights at the cemeteries.

From right to left: Aaron, Martina, Joshua and David at the gravesite of Martina's parents for Dia de Muertos celebration in Tareton, Michoachan 2005 (courtesy of Martina Gonzalez).

Grave markers of Martina Gonzalez's parents (courtesy of Martina Gonzalez).

Martina said that some of her parent's favorite foods were mole and tres leches cake and she will make those dishes to take to her parent's gravesite. Molè is a mixture of spices that can be applied directly to meat and then cooked with the meat, or mixed with water and used as a dipping sauce to meat.

MOLÈ

Mole is a spice mixture that can be made with chicken or pork. Sometimes people just make up a dry spice rub that can be put on the chicken or pork. Water or chicken broth is added and the mole cooks with the meat, making a dark, rich sauce.

Dried Chili Peppers such as:
   4 pasilla chiles
   4 mulato or guajilla peppers
   6 ancho peppers

1 large chicken or 1 boston butt pork
   (cut into large pieces)
½ cup peanuts, chopped
4 tablespoons sesame seeds
2 chopped onions
4 cloves chopped garlic
½ teaspoon ground cloves
½ teaspoon coriander seeds ground
½ teaspoon anise
Black pepper to taste
1½ ounces of unsweetened chocolate squares
4 tablespoons lard
1 pound (3 medium) tomatoes,
   peeled, seeded, and chopped
2 or 3 springs fresh coriander
1 tortilla or 1 slice toast cut up
2 cans chicken broth (undiluted)
1 teaspoon cinnamon

Brown chicken or pork pieces in skillet in lard and set aside in a dutch oven with lid. Wash dried chiles in cold water; remove veins, stems and seeds; tear them into small pieces; place in a bowl and soak them in hot water for 1 hour (about 1 cup water to 6 chiles). Now they are ready to be pureed with other spices—always include the water in which they have been soaking to the other ingredients. Combine the onions, garlic, peanuts, cloves, cinnamon, coriander seeds, anise, 2 tablespoons of the sesame seeds, coriander, tortilla or toast, prepared chiles, and the tomatoes. Using a food processor, blend the mixture, adding small amounts at a time. Cook the puree in the hot fat for 5 minutes, stirring constantly. Add the chicken broth, chocolate, salt and pepper to taste and cook until the chocolate has melted. The sauce should be very thick, like heavy cream. Pour the sauce over the chicken or pork pieces and cook covered, on low until tender (300F degrees, 2 or 3 hours until meat is tender and falls apart). Serve with hot tortillas, guacamole, frijoles and white rice.

GUACAMOLE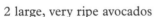

2 large, very ripe avocados
1 medium tomato, peeled, seeded and chopped
½ small onion, minced
2 or more canned Serrano chiles, chopped
Several sprigs or fresh coriander,
   finely chopped
Salt and pepper to taste
Pinch of sugar

Peel and mash the avocados. Mix well with the other ingredients and pile into a serving dish. Place one of the avocado pits in the center. This keeps the guacamole from turning brown. Refrigerate immediately and cover if you are not using right away.

Agriculture in Oldham County

The early development of Oldham County centered around agriculture and only those trades incidental and necessary to farming received attention. Farmers produced nearly everything consumed by their families and each farm was a self-contained, self-supporting economic unity. Spring, summer and fall were absorbed in plowing, seeding, cultivating, harvesting, and other fieldwork.

Grains, such as wheat and corn, were harvested and then milled or ground into flours at the local gristmills. Mills were common all over Oldham County. They were more than a place to do business, they were a day's outing and an opportunity to meet neighbors and share gossip and stories. The mills varied in size, efficiency and design, some driven by water, some by steam and others were horse powered. Grist mills were located along large creeks so that the water could power the large paddle wheels that, in turn, rotated the stone wheels that ground the grain.

Saddlers Grist Mill on Harrods Creek

This is Saddler's Mill built on Harrod's Creek by Gabriel Overstreet for Abbingdon Phelps about 1790. The mill was sold in 1830 and passed through several ownerships. The mill started as a grist mill and later served as both a grist and lumber mill. (Source: History and Families; Oldham County Kentucky).

Truck farms were common and supplied local produce to cities such as Louisville. Potatoes, tomatoes, beans, and corn were examples of major crops that were grown. Dairy and meat production were an important part of the family farm as well. At one time, Oldham County was the leader in milk production for the state of Kentucky.

Goats, chickens, hogs and beef cattle provided the staples of meat consumed. Hog killing usually took place in the cool days of fall and it took the family, relatives and neighbors to help butcher and process the meat. Hams and bacon were cured and smoked and there were several local farmers who became known for their country hams.

Work horses at Hermitage Farm circa 1920s (Oldham County Historical Society Water's Collection.

HOG KILLING TIME

Corn and pork were primary staples in every Oldham County home over the years. The hog killing was an important family and neighborhood event when people helped each other fill their pantries and smokehouses for the winter months ahead. We received many recipes and stories about hog killin', and making rubs for curing and smoking hams. These are what we thought were some of the best.

Genealogy researcher for the Oldham County History Center, Dot Carraco, relates the following story about growing up on the farm. Her family's farm was near Brownsboro, approximately where the Crestwood exit off I-71 is located today.

"Being the youngest of 8 children and living on a farm, my parents raised all the vegetables, fruit, and meat we ate. The corn and wheat were taken to the Smithfield Mill in Henry County (Our Best Restaurant today) for grinding into meal and flour. The vegetables were canned for the coming winter use. When we bought produce in season, such as peaches, we would buy 5–6 bushels to can on Saturdays. Markets would sell cheaper on Saturdays because the fruit might spoil over Sundays—that meant working up the peaches until midnight and canning. To finish up on Monday, the peaches had been sorted, the worst had been canned first. The different vegetables and fruits were canned and or preserved. These then would be stored in the cellar until used. In late summer or early fall, the variety of all the vegetables were gathered and soup mixtures were made, this I liked to help with.

Our main meat was chicken and pork, baking hens were the "culls," ones that were not laying eggs. In the spring we couldn't wait for the baby chickens to get to fryer size, about 2½ pounds. The baby chicks were purchased from Sears & Roebuck and shipped by train to Crestwood. Later they were purchased at the hatchery in Crestwood.

In the early winter, 2–3 hogs were killed for meat and lard. The weather had to be cold to keep the meat from spoiling. The hogs were killed, scalded and hung on poles, the hair scraped off and the pigs "gutted." Once cool, the hogs were cut into bacon, ham, shoulders and spare ribs. Then they trimmed off the fat and the skins were put in the big iron kettle with a good fire and lots of hot coals to render the lard to be used. Lard was all we used for frying or baking!

When the grease was done in the kettle, which took some time and had to be stirred to keep from scorching, the rinds were taken out and brought to the house to put in the lard press. The rinds were pressed to get all the grease out of them—we reserved the skins and deep fried them to make—"cracklins"—these were good munchies! All the lard would be stored in 5 gallon cans and put in the cellar. Our cellar was under the house with only an inside entrance.

The ham, shoulders and bacon were seasoned with salt, red and black pepper, sugar and salt peter. This was rubbed on the meat and let stand for 2 weeks and more was rubbed in until all was taken up—this could take up to 4 weeks or more. Then the meat was hung in the smoke house. Hickory wood was used for the smoking process.

After ham or shoulder slices were fried, the grease was left in the iron skillet and an equal amount of rich whole cream was added to the grease and let bubble good for a few minutes to mix well. Good over homemade biscuits. No gravy could ever beat this, best taste you would ever want.

Sausage meat, the lean scraps, was seasoned with salt, pepper and sage, then ground. Some sausage was canned, the rest would be smoked. To do this, one and two pound cloth bags had been made. The ground sausage meat was put in the lard press since this would press more meat tightly into the clothe bags. The bottom of the lard press had a spout on it and the clothe bags would be attached to the spout.

To can sausage meat, sausage balls were made and fried then placed in sterilized glass canning jars. Hot grease was poured over the sausage balls and the jars were sealed.

The pork tenderloins were cut into smaller pieces and seasoned with salt and pepper and placed into sterilized canning jars. A small amount of water was poured over the tenderloins in the jar. The jars were sealed and placed in a water bath canner to cook for an appropriate time. This was good eating and made good sandwich meat, also good hash with cubed potatoes, onions, canned tomatoes and water mixed with flour to thicken! All the cooking and canning was done on a large iron woodburning cookstove.

I have always said we "lived high on the hog"—our meals were breakfast, dinner and supper!"

Lard press (Oldham County Historical Society Collection).

Here is another good story about hog killing days and the Dawson Family. It is submitted by Helen McKinney who is a free lance reporter for Roundabout and she and her family are also re-enactors for the Painted Stone Settlers.

"Killing hogs was an all day process for my grandparents. The day began by killing hogs with a 22 rifle or slitting their throats. They were bled by sticking the jugular vein. Next, the carcass was scalded in a vat or tub of water (my grandparents used a metal "scalding box"). The animal's hair was scraped away and it was gutted. The heads were cut off and the body was hung on scaffolding to cool and drain.

This picture was taken in the 1940s, probably on the Edgar Rooney farm on Jericho Road, where my grandparents, Shirley and Sally Dawson, owned a farm next to his. My grandparents and Mr. Rooney raised hogs and got together each year in late November when the weather was down to the freezing point (around Thanksgiving) for a hog killin' day. (courtesy of Helen McKinney).

When ready, the body was placed on a large table or on boards (a tobacco stripping room table was often used) and divided into the desired cuts. Chops, tenderloin, hams, bacon, jowl and shoulders were taken to the smokehouse to cure. The cuts of meat were salted and rubbed with brown sugar (in old times, a mixture of red or black pepper was used to keep the bugs or "skippers" off of the meat.).

Hams and shoulders were placed in unbleached, white muslin sacks or brown paper bags. The bits and pieces that were left over were ground in a meat grinder to make sausage. My grandmother canned the sausage, patting it out into small cakes. She would heat lard and pour over the sausage. When ready to eat, she would have her grease on top of the jar for sausage gravy, to go with the sausage patties. In later years, she would freeze it, wrapping the patties in muslin first. In this way, it could be sliced just as we slice sausage rolls today.

All of the hog meat was trimmed and the fat was placed into a big iron kettle which sat outside. It was cooked slowly until the fat melted, but one had to be careful not to burn it, for this would ruin it and you would loose your year's supply of lard. Smaller pieces of scrap meat were squeezed through a lard press to get the remaining grease out. Next it was strained through a cheesecloth and poured into crocks or lard cans. It would firm up and keep for a year.

The hog's head was cleaned and put into a big pot of water and cooked until the meat fell off the bones. My grandmother used these meat bits to make mincemeat, often baking mincemeat pies. Every bit of the hog was used, including the feet, tail and pig's knuckles. Nothing was every wasted on the farm, no matter how small or useless it seemed."

Other families gave us their family photos and recipes for pork. The Bottorff's shared this old German recipe for Scrapple.

SCRAPPLE

First you take a hog's head without the brain and boil it until it falls from the bone (put in part of the hog's liver for added flavor). Drain the water off and add cornmeal to the parts to make a thick mush. Season with salt, pepper and sage. Put into loaf pans and chill. When firm it can be sliced and fried. Great for breakfast and sandwiches.

MIXTURE FOR CURING HAMS, BACONS, SHOULDERS, AND JOWL BUTTS *Submitted by Joyce McKinney*

3 pints salt
1 pound light brown sugar
1 ounce saltpeter
½ pound black pepper

Mix all ingredients together. Mixture should be rubbed generously into surfaces of meat pieces, especially into cut ends. Rub into jowl and bacon once. Rub on shoulders twice and hams three times, waiting several days between applications. Hang pieces in smokehouse for smoking. Hickory wood was preferred for smoking.

If all this "hog killin" talk doesn't make you anxious to go kill a pig, Phillip Koenig shares his mother, Kitty Koenig's easy salami recipe:

EASY SALAMI

5 lbs. cheap hamburger
5 tablespoons Morton's Quick Salt
2 ½ tablespoons Cracker Pepper
2 ½ tablespoons Mustard Seed
2 ½ tablespoons Garlic Powder
2 teaspoons Liquid Smoke

Mix all above very well and wrap in Saran Wrap in 3 loaves. Refrigerate for 24 hours. Knead again (mix well). Do this 3 days–24 hours apart. On 3rd day, cook 7–8 hours at 140 F degrees. Can be frozen and made in any size.

Another local country ham connoisseur is Joe Nay. Joe has smoked and cured hams for many years on his farm off Hwy. 42. He and his wife, Cornelia, share their recipes for Country Ham, Fried Country Ham, Red Eye Gravy and Biscuits.

Joe Nay in his smokehouse circa 1970s (courtesy Joe Nay).

Wade Hampton article (reprint with permission from the Courier-Journal, August 19, 1935.)

COUNTRY HAM

Cover ham with cold water and soak overnight. Pour off water. Place ham, skin side up, in a roaster. Fill roaster about ¾ full with cold water. Add a mixture of 2 cups brown sugar and 1 cup of vinegar. Cook in 400 F degree oven approximately 1 hour. Reduce heat to 200–250 F and simmer about 20–25 minutes per pound (bone in butt end will be loose when ham is done). Remove from oven. Allow to cool in water in which it was cooked. When cool, remove skin and trim off excess fat. Glaze—sprinkle with sugar and place in 400 degree oven about 15 minutes.

FRIED COUNTRY HAM

Slice uncooked ham about ³⁄₁₆ to ¼ thick. Trim off excess rind and dark outer edge. If desired, soak slices in milk about 1 hour before frying. Put slices in medium hot, heavy skillet. Turn several times until cooked through.

RED-EYE GRAVY

Remove fried ham from skillet and pour off excess fat, leaving the brown residue. Add enough hot water to dissolve residue and simmer about 3 minutes. Pour over fried ham slices.

Agriculture in Oldham County

ANGEL BISCUITS

5 Cups plain flour
1 teaspoon baking soda
3 teaspoons baking powder
2 tablespoons sugar
1 teaspoon salt
1 pkg. active dry yeast in ¼ cup warm water
1¼ cup shortening (Crisco)
2 cups buttermilk

Dissolve yeast in ½ cup warm water. Let stand 20 minutes. Sift flour. Add soda, baking powder, salt and sugar to flour and mix well. Cut shortening into flour and mix until fine crumbs. Add yeast and buttermilk to flour mixture. Mix with until batter is moist. Cover bowl with cloth or plastic wrap. Place in refrigerator 2 hours or overnight. Roll out lightly on floured surface to ½ inch thickness. Bake at 350 F. Degree oven for 12 minutes or until biscuits lightly browned.

POTATOES AND OLDHAM COUNTY *Submitted by Ruth Klingenfus*

In the 1930s nearly every farmer in Oldham County had ten or fifteen acres of potatoes. Harvesting potatoes from the fields was a community affair. I picked up potatoes as a young child of eight, ten, and twelve years old. You went from one farm to the next, carrying a potato basket to put them in. You took the full basket to the barrel and they gave you ten cents for a full basket. Everyone used what they had, so we ate potatoes three times a day. Times were tough, but I think that made us tougher.

GERMAN POTATO SALAD   *Submitted by Ruth Klingenfus*

My husband Carl's family was German, and I wanted to cook to please him. My recipe for German Potato Salad is one that I got from Carl's mother (Nettie Hampton Klingenfus). It has been passed down through the Klingenfus family. When we had get-togethers we always had German Potato Salad. I'm still asked to make it whenever we have a family picnic.

½ pound bacon (10 to 12 slices)
½ cup chopped onion
1 tablespoon all purpose flour
1 tablespoon sugar
1½ teaspoons celery seed
½ cup vinegar
6 cups sliced, cooked potatoes
Parsley and pimento
Bacon curls

Cook bacon until crisp; drain and crumble, reserving ¼ cup fat. Cook onion in reserved fat until tender. Blend in flour, sugar, salt, celery seed and dash of pepper. Add vinegar and 1 cup water; cook and stir until thickened and bubbly. Add bacon and potatoes; heat thoroughly, tossing lightly. Garnish with parsley, pimento and bacon curls.

Root Cellar Recipes

Root cellars were essential for food storage and preparation before the days of refrigeration and supermarkets. Built below ground level and often over freshwater springs, root cellars kept foods from spoiling in the summer and freezing in the winter. Blocks of ice could be kept cold for several months, (usually blanketed with layers of straw), and the humidity levels were ideal for keeping "root" vegetables from rotting throughout the winter. Even cured meats, like ham and bacon, could be kept in root cellars as long as the temperature was 40 degrees or below. The root cellar at the Oldham County History Center has been restored and was built in 1840. It is now being used to educate visitors about the ways people used to recycle and conserve their resources.

Restored root cellar at the Oldham County History Center (staff photo)

Interior of root cellar at the Oldham County History Center (staff photo)

SAUERKRAUT *Submitted by Mrs. G. D. Ripley*

Shred cabbage and tamp down very firmly into sterilized 1 quart jars. Put 1 heaping teaspoons of salt on top of cabbage and fill jars with boiling water (be sure there are no air bubbles). Seal jars with rubbers and zinc tops. Immediately store jars at room temperature.

PICKLED GREEN BEANS *Submitted by Mrs. G. D. Ripley*

7 lbs of green beans
3 lbs of sugar
1 quart of vinegar
A little mixed spice if preferred

Boil beans in salt water until tender and then drain. Make a syrup of vinegar and sugar and add beans. Bring to a boil. Fill sterilized canning jars with the mixture and seal. This is a sweet pickle.

CUCUMBER PICKLES *Miss Lilah Hembree, County Extension Agent*

Miss Lilah Hembree was the home extension agent in the 1950s and 1960s in Oldham County. She taught numerous classes on sewing and cooking in both 4-H and with local homemaker groups She is fondly remembered for her many years of service and activities that she gave to the women and children of Oldham County.

To make brine for pickles do not use table salt, use coarse or pickling salt. For brine make up 1 pint salt to 9 quarts of water or until brine will barely float a new laid egg.

Put whole cucumbers in brine, use a board or plate to keep cucumbers under water—not too heavily weighted. At the end of each week put ½ cup (pint) of salt on plate for 5 to 6 weeks. Skim off scum as it forms.

Take pickles out of brine. Soak for 24 hours.

Dilute vinegar ½ with water and add 1 tablespoon of alum. Add cucumbers cut in small pieces. Bring to a boiling point and keep there until pickles are firm. Drain cucumbers and add this mixture 3½ pounds of sugar to 1 quart of vinegar—add 1 teaspoon of pickling spices. Use this mixture for every 7 pounds of pickles. Heat to boiling and pour over cucumbers every morning for 7 mornings. Pack in sterilized jars and seal. To see that pickles are firm, prick with fingers.

CANNED STRAWBERRIES

Taken from Louise King's recipes, 1938, submitted by Joyce McKinney

Make thin syrup as follows:
1 cup water
1 cup sugar
Boil for 5 minutes

Put strawberries in boiling syrup as many as will take up syrup and boil 2 minutes. Let stand overnight. Next morning bring to a boil, pack in hot, sterile jars, process in simmering water for 8 minutes. Seal tightly.

SWEET PICKLES   *taken from Louise King's recipes, 1938, submitted by Joyce McKinney*

To 7 pounds of fruit (watermelon, cantaloupe rind, or cucumbers) take 3 pounds of sugar and 1 pint vinegar. Let the vinegar and sugar come to a boil, then drop in the fruit and cook until tender.

Season to taste and process in clean, sterilized jars. Process in boiling water bath for 8 minutes. Seal tightly.

PICKLED EGGPLANT   *Submitted by Joyce Keibler*

This recipe was given to me by my Italian friend's mother, it was written in Italian and then translated.

Eggplants (as many extra's you have
    at end of summer growing season)
2 cups white vinegar
1 cup water
Red peppers, cloves of garlic, sliced
Black pepper
Oregano
Sweet basil
Fresh parsley, chopped
Mint leaves sliced
Olive oil

Peel and slice eggplant about the size of cucumbers. Layer slices with salt in glass dish. Press with a pan of water and sit overnight. In morning, squeeze water out of eggplant slices.

Boil 2 cups white vinegar and 1 cup water. Boil eggplant slices (about 10–12 at a time) until the eggplant looks creamy or milky in color. Drain in colander—continue until all slices are done. Place layers of eggplant in a large bowl, alternating with spices (garlic, peppers, etc) cover with olive oil. Let sit in bowl for 1 hour.

Place mixture in sterilized jars. Refrigerate. Serve as appetizer or in a Italian sub sandwich.

THE LIBERTY SCHOOL CANNERY

Long time resident and farmer, Ann Dick, shares this story and pickle recipe she received from one of her neighbors, Bernice Bottorff:

In the 1940s, Liberty Elementary School was nearly as busy in the summer as during the school term in the 1940s. Ladies from all around brought their garden vegetables to the cannery. The vegetables and fruits were picked, washed, snapped and cut-up at home and taken to the cannery for blanching and canning. Huge stainless steel vats were used for blanching the food. After blanching, the food was then transferred into quart or pint-size tins and sealed. The cans were processed by steam. We were charged a minimal fee, maybe 7 to 10 cents.

BERNICE BOTTORFF'S DILL PICKLES   *Submitted by Ann Dick*

Sterilize pint jars and place in each jar: 1 clove garlic, 1 flower head of dill or 1 teaspoon of dill weed. Scrub cucumbers and slice and pack into the jars.

Bring to a boil:
>   2 quarts white vinegar
>   1 quart water
>   1 cup coarse salt
>   ½ teaspoon alum

Pour this boiling hot mixture over the cucumbers in each jar. Seal. Allow to ripen before using (several weeks). When opened, keep in refrigerator.

CANNED PORK TENDERLOIN   *Submitted by Jan Morgan*

I learned how to home-can pork from my mother, Aline Branstetter, on the farm near Horse Cave, Ky. Our entire family treasured this delicious tenderloin and it was usually saved for special occasions, such as Christmas morning. In my opinion, there is nothing as delicious as this tenderloin and the accompanying white gravy made with the natural juices that came from the bottom of the quart jar. To this day, my brother and I reminisce about this yummy meat and gravy and long to have it for family gatherings again. In my mother's later years, even when there was no hog killing, she would purchase tenderloin from the store and home-can 3 or 4 jars just so we could enjoy it for special occasions

After the hog was butchered, the leanest part of the tenderloin was removed and cut into slices about 1 to 2 inches thick. Next, one would tightly pack these slices/pieces into quart jars. (I often got this packing job because my young-girl hands were smaller than my mom's). Then a small amount of water (approximately ½ cup) was added to the jar of meat. The jars were sealed with jar lids and rims and placed into my grandmother's pressure cooker (and I still use this cooker today for my vegetable canning!). Enough water was put into the pressure cooker so that the jars were sitting about threes inches deep. Then the lid was clamped and screwed down very tightly with the steam shuttle open. When the steam would begin spewing from the shuttle-cock, the escape valve was closed and the pressure cooker continued to build up pressure. When the pressure reached 10 pounds, the burner was adjusted to maintain that pressure for approximately 50 minutes to one hour. Then the burner would be turned off, allowing the pressure cooker to cool and the pressure to go back to zero. Next, the shuttle-cock was opened to let off the small amount of remaining steam. Then, and only then, could we open the lid and remove the jars of beautiful pink tenderloin bubbling in its own juices.

DAIRIES

As one of the top diary producing counties in Kentucky, Oldham County families had lots of recipes with milk. Here are some of the different ways that families made use of all that milk and cream!

MILK, CREAM AND OYSTERS

During the 1920s and later, fresh oysters were available for purchase only around Christmas in Oldham County. Oyster soup and scalloped oysters were two of the most popular dishes that were served (and still are!). Today you can get gallons of fresh oysters in the shell at Clem's Seafood in Buckner where they are shipped in on Thursdays from Apalachacola Bay, Florida.

Norman E. Dick, Jr. with mother delivering milk to town, 1923 (Oldham County Historical Society Collection)

OYSTER SOUP *Submitted by the Dick Family*

1 pint fresh oysters, drained
½ cup butter
2 cups milk + ½ cup cream and part of the oyster liquor
Salt and pepper to taste

Separate oysters from oyster liquor. Melt butter in pan or skillet at medium temperature. Add oysters and sauté until oysters curl around edges. Add the milk/cream/oyster liquor and heat to very hot (do not overheat as the mixture will curdle). Add salt and pepper to taste and serve.

MILK AND EGGS

Of course another classic milk recipe is one with eggs—custards, ice creams, rich egg sauces, are the result of some delicious combinations. The following recipe is submitted by Kathleen Woolfolk in memory of her mother, Florence Smiser. Kathleen writes: "We always had boiled custard with whipped cream on top for our Christmas dinner. One year my mother was late in getting the custard made and set it on top of the rain barrel which had a thick coating of ice on top to cool. When she went to serve the custard for dinner, it was at the bottom of the rain barrel!"

FLORENCE'S BOILED CUSTARD

3 cups whole milk
2 large eggs
¼ teaspoon salt
¾ cup sugar
½ teaspoon vanilla

Heat milk in double boiler over hot water. Beat eggs until light and foamy. Gradually beat in sugar and salt. Add the hot milk slowly over egg and sugar mixture, beating constantly. Return to double boiler and cook until mixture coats a spoon. Add vanilla. Cooking at low temperature is the secret of making velvet smooth custard. We always served it in glasses with whipped cream on top.

VEGETABLE GARDENS

Up until recent years, almost every family in Oldham County had a garden. Heirloom vegetables were grown year after year—heirloom varieties are those plants that have been passed down from generation to generation over the years. Many heirlooms are considered pioneer plants that people brought with them when they migrated from Europe or Africa. Most people would save their seeds from their favorite plants to re-plant for the next year.

The following excerpt is taken from an article in the Oldham Era written by Paul Gottbrath, April 8, 1976

An easy-moving 73, Alen Coons has been gardening for most of his years, the last 32 of them on the half-acre lot behind his house on Washington Street in LaGrange. Last year's harvest was typical he says. "We had tomatoes running out our ears, nose, and mouth, enough lima beans to sell 11 gallons we had left over, and corn that we still haven't gotten rid of. Had some trouble with the cabbage though," he adds with a wink. "Couldn't get a head over nine pounds!"

Coons is a firm believer in the soundness of many age-old gardening axioms. He spurns commercial fertilizer, for instance, preferring to let cover crops such as red clover replenish the soil when he's not using it. "I only use half my yard at one time," he explains, "and I leave the other half in clover for three years at a time. When I'm ready to use it again, that clover's given it everything it needs."

He also disdains mechanized means to prepare his soil, opting instead to use his own back behind a hoe, rake or spade. "Plowing with a machine leaves hard streaks in it," he says. "When I get through using a spade on it there's not a hard streak to be found."

And he observes the dictates of the moon in planting his garden. He says the basic rule of thumb in lunar planting is to sew vegetables that grow beneath the surface—root crops such as potatoes, turnips, and carrots—during a period of "dark moon" (the full moon and the last quarter).

Surface crops are best planted when the moon is "light" (first quarter and the new moon).

Coons says he doesn't know how the method works, but has been using it for years and believes in it. "I know a lot of people will laugh at this, but I go by it and I prosper by it," he declared.

YELLOW SQUASH CASSEROLE *Submitted by Jeanne Gibson and Minnie Lee Brooks*

1 quart yellow squash, sliced
   (can use both yellow and zucchini)
1 medium onion grated
1 can of cream of mushroom soup
1 cup grated cheddar cheese
Salt and pepper to taste
Cheese crackers, crushed

Cook squash in boiling water until crisp and tender, drain well. Mix onion, soup, salt and pepper. Grease casserole dish. Layer squash and soup mixture. Top with cheese and crackers. Bake at 375 F degrees for 30 minutes.

CORN FRITTERS *Submitted by Dot Carraco*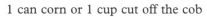

1 can corn or 1 cup cut off the cob
1 teaspoon baking powder
2 teaspoons salt
2 eggs
½ cup flour

Add dry ingredients mixed and sifted well to corn. Then add beaten egg yolks and fold in whites. Drop the mixture by the tablespoon into deep fat and brown.

HEIRLOOM TOMATOES

The history center grows heirloom variety tomatoes each summer on the grounds. They are provided by volunteer Gary Millwood who has become a local expert on various varieties of heirloom tomatoes. Gary is a retired chef now and shares some of his favorite tomato recipes.

FRESH TOMATO PASTA   *Submitted by Gary Millwood*

2 cups seeded and diced ripe tomato
3 tablespoons minced sweet onion
1 clove garlic, mashed
¼ cup of basil or Italian parsley, thinly sliced
¼ teaspoon marjoram
2 tablespoons olive oil
Dash of salt

Dash of cracked pepper
4 cups of hot cooked pasta.
Grated cheese

Prepare vegetables and seasonings and combine them in a large bowl. Add hot pasta and toss to combine. Sprinkle with cheese.

TOMATO PIE   *Submitted by Gary Millwood*

1 baked 8 or 9 inch pie crust

Filling for pie:
5 to 6 medium tomatoes, peeled and
     sliced about ½ inch thick; place in
     colander to drain
2 to 3 tablespoons fresh chopped basil
Salt, pepper and garlic powder to taste
1¼ cup cheddar cheese
     (sometime I use a mixture of cheddar,
     Colby and Monterey Jack)
¾ cup mayonnaise

Layer ½ tomatoes in baked pie shell. Sprinkle ½ basil, salt, pepper, garlic powder on top. Repeat. Mix cheese and mayonnaise together and spread over tomato layers, right to inside edge of crust.

Bake at 350 F degrees for 30 minutes or until topping is golden brown.

ANITA SPRINGS

After the Revolutionary War, Lt. John Russell of Henrico, VA received a land grant of 3,000 acres in the vicinity of LaGrange among which were five natural limestone spring waters. As the land grant was sold and split into smaller acreages, 200 acres became known as "Anita Springs" in 1877 when it became the home of Dr. James Thornley Berry who married Anita Anderson Gray of Louisville in 1877. The site was described as "Five springs, surrounded by lovely green hills, the long slopes of which are dotted with fine old trees and with a view of extended loveliness away down the valley and far out over the hills, reposeful and inspiring". [source: History and Families: Oldham County Kentucky, pp. 195–196]. In 1894 Dr. Berry started the Anita Water Company, bottling the mineral spring water and shipping it to Louisville via the L&N Railroad Company.

The Royal Inn was located close to Anita Springs at the end of Kentucky Avenue in LaGrange.

Royal Inn located near Anita Springs in LaGrange (Oldham County History Center Collection)

This lemonade recipe was a favorite of Maude Varble. Shelby and Maude had a grocery over on Covington Ridge and later bought a farm on north Hwy. 53 where they raised sheep and chickens. Behind the hill down from their farmhouse there was a cold spring that ran from the limestone outcroppings under the shade of locust and sycamore trees. Shelby would bring up the fresh water from the spring for Maude's lemonade. Maude would make up her lemonade in batches and serve it in the hot summer afternoons under her grape arbor for her neighbors.

MAUDE VARBLE'S LEMONADE   *Submitted by Nancy Theiss*

2 cups sugar
2 cups water
2 cups of freshly squeezed lemon juice

Boil sugar and water together until sugar dissolves. Let cool. Add 2 cups of lemon juice. Chill. Pour over chopped ice in glasses. Put in a sprig of fresh mint if desired.

Agriculture in Oldham County

WINE COUNTRY

At the turn of the Twentieth Century, many Oldham County farms cultivated grape arbors and produced commercial wine that was shipped to Louisville, Cincinnati and other cities. Of course, many families produced wine and other "brew" for their own consumption. Many of these cultivar grapes were carried from German and English families that immigrated to Oldham County during the 19th Century. The following stories provide images of our wine producing heritage from the old countries of Europe.

Otto Dilly's family lived in a picturesque, two story white framed home in Buckner close to the south side of the railroad tracks. His father was Otto Friedrich Klosterman (1840–1918) who married Johanna Henriette Lefevre (1845–1915). Otto Dilly's great grandparents operated a winery at Buckner for some years; they had a vineyard of their own but also bought grapes from farmers in the area. Otto's grandmother, Addie Klosterman Dilly (1872–1955) shared this story with her grandson.

Klosterman family at Buckner circa 1905 from left to right: Franz Julius Lefevre, Otto Freidrich Klosterman, Topsy (former slave, not family's), Otto Lefevre Dilly, Addie Marie Klosterman, Johanna Henriette Lefevre, Meta Mary Klosterman, Beno Joseph Klosterman (courtesy of Otto and Jane Dilly).

Klosterman Home near railroad tracks in Buckner circa 1905 (courtesy of Otto and Jane Dilly).

"The L&N railroad track was in front of the Buckner house, with a side track in the same location, the side track was used to shunt trains there in order to let express trains go by. A troop train was side-tracked there full of Spanish American War soldiers. My great grandmother, Johanna Henriette Klosterman, asked the commanding officer if they could treat the "boys" with some wine. He said alright, but probably with some regrets, since after several kegs of wine there was a whole train full of too happy soldiers, including the engineer, consequently delaying the train for nearly four hours!"

The Mount Family shares the following recipes for wine, home brew and blackberry cordial. Craig Mount claims his grandparents did all their wine and brew making and drinking at the home of T. T. Clausen near Goshen. T. T.'s sister, Mary doesn't remember it that way!

ELDERBERRY WINE *Mary Trigg Mount (1881–1959)*

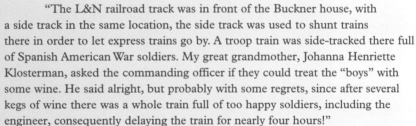

1 quart elderberry flowers
9 lbs sugar
3 gallons water
½ cup lemon juice
1 cake compressed yeast
4 packages of 1 lb raisins

Pick blossoms from stems and pack a quart measure tight. Put sugar and water on fire and when boiling, add blossoms then simmer five minutes. Let cool and pour into earthenware crock. When lukewarm add lemon juice and yeast. Cover with cheese cloth or crock top. Stir everyday, three times for six days. The seventh day divide each package of raisins into ¼ package and place in a quart mason jar (You will have sixteen quart jars). Strain the wine into each of the jars and cap tight for six months.

BLACKBERRY CORDIAL *Mary Trigg Mount (1881–1959)*

To one quart of blackberry juice, add one pound of white sugar, one tablespoon each of cloves, allspice, nutmeg and cinnamon. Boil all this together for 15 minutes and add a wine glassful of brandy whiskey and bring to simmer. Bottle while hot, cork tight and seal.

HOME BREW *Letty Mount (1906-1998)*

Put hops in a sack into a kettle of cold water and boil for about 10 minutes. Add malt and two pounds of brown sugar to the boiling water and boil this mixture for about 10 minutes. Cool and pour into a 6 gallon jar, adding enough water to make 5 gallons. When the mixture is lukewarm, take out the sack of hops and add 1 cake of yeast and 1 teaspoon of salt. Cover and let this mixture stand for 72 hours. Pour into pint jars, adding ¼ teaspoon of sugar into each jar—makes 45 pints.

BEER MUFFINS *Submitted by Phillip Koenig from Mother Kitty's recipes*

3 cups self-rising flour
¼ sugar
1 can cold beer

Grease muffin tins or use paper cups. Mix well and bake at 350 F degrees for 40–45-minutes.

The Bottorff's, who live in the same area of the county as the Mount's, have their own family wine method they have shared:

BOTTORFF FAMILY WINE
Submitted by Polly Bottorff Miller

To each gallon of grape juice add 2 lbs of sugar. Pour into clean plastic buckets or crocks. Put in a cool area such as a basement or root cellar. Skim foam from the crocks each day until it quits working (the foam stops). Drink then, or, bottle and cork. Let age 6 months to a year (time in between doesn't have much taste). There is no added yeast to this wine.

Albert Bottoroff using his wine press on farm (courtesy of Polly Bottorff Miller).

BOURBON AND BRANCH

The Oldham County History Center has one of the largest whiskey jug collections in the United States. These jugs were donated by J. Chilton Barnett and they can be seen on the history center website: oldhamcountyhistoricalsociety.org. The jugs are ceramic and were available up to Prohibition. The combination of fresh spring branch water and the abundance of corn raised on farms made moonshine a popular product to sell. Almost every Kentucky family in the past participated in or had family members who sold moonshine—it was an important supplemental income. Moonshine was produced by individuals and sold to local saloons, groceries, hotels, etc. People would buy their jugs and have them refilled at various establishments. These jugs served as advertisements for these businesses. After prohibition the government took the business into retail so that the ceramic jugs were replaced by bottles and mass produced by industries. There were always good stories about moonshiners and tales of near "misses" by revenue agents who sought out illegal production.

Carlos Knight, who grew up in Oldham County during the first half of the 20th century remembers, as a boy, helping to deliver moonshine, across the river to the Indiana side. He said the reason Hurricane Holler got its name (near Westport) is because moonshiners used hurricane lanterns to signal across the river during the night, when a pick-up was ready. Today, there are families in Oldham County that are associated with 2 of the biggest distillers in Kentucky, Brown-Forman and Maker's Mark. Phillip Koenig, native Oldham Countian and co-owner of Silver Spoon Catering shares some of his favorite bourbon recipes!!

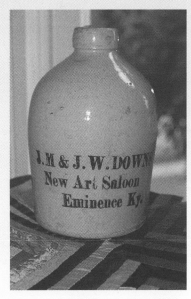

Application for Intoxicating Liquor (Oldham County History Center Collection).

One of the 467 rare whiskey jugs in the Oldham County History Center Collection, staff photo).

New Art Saloon Jug (Oldham County History Center Collection, staff photo).

MANDARIN ORANGE MARINADE *Submitted by Phillip Koenig*

Use for any type of meat, fish, poultry.

2 cups soy sauce
1½ cups red wine vinegar
1½ cups Jim Beam bourbon
2 cups concentrated orange juice
1 cup Hoisin sauce (bottled commercially)
4 cups sugar (superfine if available)

Mix ingredients together. Add meat and marinate for a minimum of 12 hours.

VIDALIA ONION PIE *Submitted by Phillip Koenig*

2 pounds onions, thinly sliced
1 stick butter
3 eggs, well beaten
1 cup sour cream
¼ teaspoon salt
¼ teaspoon white pepper
¼ teaspoon Tabasco sauce
2 9-inch pastry shells
4 tablespoons bourbon
Grated Parmesan Cheese

Bake pie shells at 350 F degrees for 8 minutes. Saute onions in butter. Combine eggs, sour cream and seasonings. Add to sautéed onion. Pour mixture in pastry shells. Top with Parmesan Cheese. Bake at 350 F degrees for 20 minutes, then 325 F degrees for 15 minutes or until slightly browned.

COUNTRY HAM AND GRUYERE TARTS *Submitted by Phillip Koenig*

½ pound chopped country ham
1 medium onion, diced
8 ounces of chopped pimentos
1 pound of cream cheese
½ pound Grated Gruyere Cheese
Salt and pepper to taste
1 package refrigerated Pillsbury Pie Dough
  for tart shells

Sauté onions until golden brown. Add remaining ingredients and shape into walnut sized balls. Place small pieces of dough into miniature tart pans and place one of the filling balls in each tart. Bake at 350 F degrees for 15–18 minutes. Cool and remove from tart pans. Serve warm.

BOURBON PATE   *Submitted by Phillip Koenig*

1 (¼" thick) sliced boiled ham, about ½ pound
1 (¼" thick) slice veal, about ½ pound
½ pound salt pork
1 shallot (or green onion) minced
1 bay leaf
½ teaspoon thyme
4 tablespoons bourbon
2 pounds lean ground pork
1 teaspoon salt
⅛ teaspoon pepper
Slice bacon

Cut ham slice into ¼" strips. Trim veal edges and remove any fat. Cut into ¼" strips. Cut salt pork into ⅛" thick slices and then cut into ⅛" strips. Put shallots, bay leaf, thyme and bourbon into flat dish. Add the meat strips and marinate 6 hours, or overnight. Mix pork, salt and pepper. Refrigerate both.

When ready to make pate, line a 4 cup mold or 2 small molds, with bacon slices. Drain liquid from meat strips into the sausage. Repeat layers until meats and sausage are used, ending with sausage. Cover top of mold with bacon slices. Cut the slices to fit, press down firmly in the mold. Cover tightly with foil and set old into a water bath. Bake at 325F degrees for two hours.

When done, take from oven, set mold into a pie pan to catch the fat and weight the pate down in the mold. (Use a quart jar or other container filled with water and closed tight or wrap a brick in foil or improvise!) The pate must be pressed while warm. When cool, refrigerate with weight. When cold, turn out of mold and scrape off the congealed fat. Save to cook with, as it has a good flavor.

Slice the pate thin and serve with pickles.

Events

WEDDINGS

This photo was from a wedding at Duncan Memorial Chapel in the early 1960s. Wedding traditions are quite varied today but this list and recipe for Champagne Punch goes back to the late 1800s from the history center collection. The food list is taken from the David Weller Collection donated by J. C. Barnett.

Wedding at Duncan Memorial Chapel circa 1960 (Oldham County History Center Collection).

Volunteer researcher, Nina Brehm has been working on these letters for the history center for the last year. The David F. C. Weller family lived in the Louisville area and the items (mainly letters) date from 1858 through 1941. The majority of the letters were written to David F. C. Weller or his wife Mary Emma (Molly) Fowler.

David was a Private in the Kentucky Infantry, 2nd

Picnic at Kavanaugh Center in Crestwood circa 1905 (Oldham County History Center Collection).

Regiment of the Confederate Volunteer army. His unit was part of what was later called the "Orphaned Brigade" because Kentucky declined to join the Confederacy and supported the Union cause. After the war he resumed his career as a "printer" at the Courier-Journal. By 1868 he joined the Kentucky "Helm Guard", an organization (like the National Guard today) of volunteer soldiers.

Researcher Nina Brehm found this menu list in the Weller Collection. We think Mary Emma was preparing for one of her daughter's weddings, either Carrie or Margaret. Carrie married George Washington Wiseman and they had nine children. Margaret married Joseph LeCoste Brown in 1912 and they had 2 children.

WELLER WEDDING MENU LIST (EARLY 1900S)

Cold ham sliced	Figs
Cold veal sliced	Assorted Cakes
Chicken salad	Wedding Cake
Salmon salad	Pink and
Lettuce	White Cake
Sardines	Coconut Cake
Pickle mix	Dolly Vardin
Cheese	Cake
Bread	Plain White
Coffee	Cake
Bananas	2 Fruit Cakes
Tropical snow	Chocolate Cake
or ambrosia	Ice Cream
Oranges	Wine
Grapes	Lemonade

This 1890 recipe was found in Rachel Townes' file by her daughter, Lucy Clausen.

CHAMPAGNE PUNCH TO SERVE 600–650

½ pound green tea (makes 10 quarts)
10 bottles brandy
10 bottles light rum
5 dozen lemons
12 pounds sugar
12 quarts carbonated water (I will use more)
12 quarts champagne
1 quart maraschino cherries
2 cans pineapple chunks

Make syrup of the sugar with 1 quart of water and boil until slightly thick, add the juice from the pineapple chunks and let come to a boil. To make tea, bring 10 quarts of water to a boil and pour onto tea; let stand until strong, then strain and when cool add syrup, rum, brandy, juice of lemons, cherries and pineapple chunks. Make this at least 5 days before using. Chill stock and champagne and when ready to serve mix 3 quarts of stock to 1 quart of champagne and 1 quart carbonated water (Three quarts of carbonated water used for Ladie's punch). Stock should be kept in tightly corked bottles)

CONTESTS

Dairylicious Pasta Dishes Recipe Contest

Ruth Heyser, once the co-owner with her husband Ted, of Chicken Trail Inn, placed second in this statewide contest sponsored by the American Dairy Association of Kentucky in 1988. Twelve contestants competed in this state cook-off that was held at the University of Kentucky at Erikson Hall. All recipes submitted had to be for a main dish containing at least three real dairy products such as milk, cream, half and half, sour cream, cheese, yogurt and butter.

RUTH'S AWARD WINNING SOUTHERN STYLE NOODLES

1 package of ½ inch wide noodles
1 tablespoon melted butter
½ cup chopped, blanched almonds
1 tablespoon poppy seeds
1 tablespoon grated orange rind
1 tablespoon grated lemon rind
½ teaspoon salt
Pepper
½ cup plain yogurt
1 cup sour cream

Cook noodles in the quantity of water recommended, adding 2–3 tablespoons of vegetable oil and two teaspoons of salt. Cook to al dente (7–10 minutes) and drain.

Mix all other ingredients EXCEPT the sour cream. Toss in noodles. Serve with dollops of sour cream on top. 4–6 servings

My First Microwave
Submitted by Patty Nuermberger

In the spring of 1979 the Oldham Era sponsored their First Annual Cookbook Contest. The grand prize for each of the three categories, Main Dish, Breads and Desserts—was a new microwave oven. Microwave ovens were still a novelty then—a new "cutting edge" appliance in the market place. I didn't have one and had never even used one. Imagine my surprise—and joy—when my name was announced as the Grand Prize winner in the Desserts category! The recipe was one my husband and I really enjoyed; Toasted Coconut Ice Cream. It's hard to remember now how large and heavy those first microwave ovens were. I had to have help to get it out of my car and into the kitchen! It had only 1 knob that you turned "on" to the required number of minutes, and there was no carousel. At first I used it only to heat water and to warm left-overs, but it gradually became part of almost every meal's preparation. I can't imagine cooking without one now!

Newspaper article (courtesy of the Oldham Era, April 12, 1979).

TOASTED COCONUT ICE CREAM

14½ ounce can (1⅔ cup) evaporated milk
½ cup sugar
2 teaspoons vanilla
1 cup whipping cream, whipped
⅓ cup flaked coconut, toasted

In saucepan, combine milk and sugar; cook and stir until sugar dissolves. Cook; stir in vanilla. Pour into 11 by 7 by 1½ inch pan. Freeze until firm. Place in a cold bowl, breaking mixture into chunks; beat smooth. Fold in whipped cream and coconut. Freeze. Makes 8 servings.

1939 Egg Meal Menu Contest Winner *From article August 4, 1939, Oldham Era*

Mrs. Alonzo Broyles of the Poplar Grove Club left Saturday for Cleveland to participate in the "cook-off" of the Egg Meal Menu Contest sponsored by the World Poultry Congress convening in Cleveland this week. In the preliminary contest the best five menus from each state in the Union were selected. From all the preliminary winners the World Poultry Congress Committee chose the best twenty. Mrs. Broyles was among these twenty winners, all of whom are in Cleveland this week for the "cook-off" which they prepare their winning menu. The top price is $1,000.

Note: Mrs. Broyles is now deceased so we talked to her sons, John and Roy. They were both vaguely familiar with the event. They recalled that her scalloped egg casserole was a part of the menu. We checked with the Poplar Grove Homemakers Club where Mrs. Broyles had been a member but could not locate the recipe or menu.

Louise's Girl Scout Broccoli Casserole *Submitted by Lucy Waters Clausen*

Louise Clausen preparing Girl Scout recipe (courtesy of Lucy Waters Clausen).

My daughter, Louise Clausen, decided to enter the Girl Scout Cook Off in 1979 or 1980. She decided to make broccoli casserole from her grandmother's recipe. Her grandmother had gotten the recipe from her friend Margaret Burge. Louise made two minor changes in the recipe and won 2nd place at the state level. She now hates to cook and this is one of the few things she will bring to family dinners.

20 ounces chopped broccoli, cooked and drained
1 can cream of chicken soup
1 cup sharp cheddar cheese, grated
2 eggs beaten well
1 cup mayonnaise (no substitutions!)
1 tablespoon grated onion
Salt and pepper to taste
½ cup buttered bread crumbs

Spread broccoli evenly in a 9x13" casserole. Mix soup, eggs, cheese, mayonnaise, and onion together and spread evenly over the broccoli. Sprinkle the bread crumbs on the top. Bake at 400 degrees for 20 minutes.

GRANNY'S OATMEAL PIE *Submitted by Sue Conn*

This recipe was handed down from my Granny Frasier and my mom (Aline Branstetter) in Horse Cave, Ky. It is one of the best and easiest pie recipes that they used. My granny always baked cakes and pies and entered them in the Horse Cave Community Fairs. And I was thrilled as a little girl to see her smile when she won many blue ribbons for her baking and cooking.

2 eggs, beaten
½ cup melted butter or margarine
⅔ cup sugar
⅔ cup white corn syrup
⅔ cup uncooked oats
¼ teaspoon salt
1 teaspoon vanilla extract
1 unbaked pie shell

Mix all ingredients together well and pour into pie shell. Bake at 350F degrees for 45 minutes to 1 hour (until light brown on top). I sometimes add ⅔ cup pecans to pie filling.

CARROT CAKE WITH CREAM CHEESE FROSTING *Submitted by Sue Conn*

I entered this recipe in the Kentucky State Fair and won fourth place. It was funny to notice when we went to the fair to see if I had won, my cake was the only one with two slices taken from it. Someone must have liked it a little better than the others!!

Carrot Cake
1½ cup vegetable oil
2 cups sugar
4 eggs

In a large bowl beat above until golden yellow.

Sift together:
2 cups flour
2½ teaspoons cinnamon
2 teaspoons baking soda
1 teaspoon salt

Add flour mixture to sugar mixture, beat 2 minutes by hand. Add following to mixture and blend until just mixed:

2½ teaspoons vanilla
3 cups grated carrots
½ cup golden raisins
½ cup chopped pecans
½ cup crushed pineapple (not drained)

Preheat oven to 325F degrees. Grease and flour three 8 inch round cake pans. Divide mixture evenly among prepared pans. Bake for 45 minutes. Cook in pan on wire rack for 10 minutes before turning onto wire rack to cool completely. Frost with cream cheese icing.

Cream Cheese Icing
Allow ¼ pound (1 stick) butter and 1 8-ounce package of cream cheese to soften at room temperature (do not use microwave to soften as it will break down ingredients). Beat together in small bowl with electric mixer and then add 1 pound of powdered sugar, 1 tablespoon vanilla and a dash of salt. Beat until blended, add a little milk for spreading consistency if necessary.

Fourth of July

Submitted by Nancy Stearns Theiss

We moved to our farm on Hwy. 53 in 1954 and it had several springs and nice ponds. One pond was spring fed from an old limestone spring house. Dad had the bank enlarged and the pond drained so when it refilled, it was without fish and always full of fresh clean spring water. Friends and family added a sand bank, dock and diving board. Dwight Freeman, who owned Freeman Ready Mix on Fendley Mill Road, put up a nice shelter and Dad moved the old outhouse from our farmhouse close to the pond so we had all the

Partygoers at the Fourth of July at "The Pond" circa 1975 (courtesy of Nancy Stearns Theiss).

conveniences! I think we began our first Fourth of July pig roast around 1956, although I am not sure—however since the "Fifties" our family has had many celebrations at "The Pond" and Fourth of July was always the highlight. Most of the families that came were local families, the Cassadys, Freemans, Radcliffes, Theisses, Dicks, Clores, Manbys, Guytons, Taylors, Armstrongs, and the Blows and Dobbins from Louisville.

In the 50's and 60's there was actually a pig "slaughtered" for the event. Although we didn't raise pigs there were plenty of people back then that did. I think Dad and Dwight always managed to get the pig—there were a few times the pig got "loose" but it always was caught! Dwight had a large rectangular frame built and the pig was split and halved down the middle and stretched out on the frame. Lu Freeman always made a "sop" to slap on the pig while it was cooking which took all day back at the pond. There were a few times when the pig caught fire, due to the negligence of the cookers, who may have had too much libation with their branch water, but somehow, the pig always tasted great. The fireworks show, I thought as a child back then, was spectacular! They were not lavish or long lasting, but they sparkled in the reflection of the pond, along with the flashing of the fireflies over the field.

Fourth of July at "The Pond", circa 1975, left to right: Joe Stearns, Lucille Freeman and Winn Stearns (courtesy of Nancy Stearns Theiss).

I do remember one particular Fourth, when my brother, Joe Brock and friend, Chuckie Dobbins, who were around 15 years old at the time, decided they would add to the food dishes by mixing up rattlesnake onion dip and grasshopper brownies. Chuckie had found a speciality story with canned grasshoppers and canned rattlesnake meat. They disappeared during the party up to the farmhouse and made their "creations" then carefully placed them onto the picnic table full of potluck dishes. Of course, they didn't tell anyone the ingredients until all was eaten. People were "picking" grasshopper legs from their teeth for the rest of the night (or at least imagined it!!). These are some of the wonderful dishes that people always brought for the Fourth.

MARTHA MANBY'S POTATO SALAD

8 potatoes
4 boiled eggs
½ to 1 jar small pimentos
½ to ¾ large sweet onion
Salt
Mayonnaise
Add celery if you like, I prefer without.

Boil the potatoes for 20 minutes, let cool. Add the rest of the ingredients, adding enough mayonnaise so potatoes are very moist. I think it is better if eaten before refrigeration.

WINN STEARNS' BOSTON BAKED BEANS

1 pound navy beans
½ pound salt pork
1 medium onion quartered
½ cup brown sugar
⅓ cup molasses
2 teaspoons dry mustard
2 teaspoons salt
¼ teaspoon pepper
2 tablespoons vinegar
2 cups hot water

Soak beans overnight in 6 cups cold water and ¼ teaspoon baking soda if water is hard. Parboil beans 20 minutes. Drain after parboiling and rinse in cold water. Dice rind of salt pork to 1 inch squares, placing in bottom of a 2 quart bean pot (or casserole with lid), along with quartered onion. Add beans. Mix remaining ingredients with hot water. Pour over beans. Top with remaining salt pork. Cover and bake in slow 300 F degree oven for 6 hours, adding water as needed to keep beans moist.

NANCY'S BEER CHEESE

1 pound sharp cheese (hand grated)
2 cloves smashed garlic
4 ounces bleu cheese
1 stick butter
½ teaspoon or more (to taste)
    of cayenne pepper
Some shakes of Worcestershire
2 tablespoons wine vinegar

Mix the above together and then open a can of beer to moisten and keep the cheese together; add enough beer so that the cheese is a spreading consistency. Drink the rest of the beer! Then put cheese in a container and let rest overnight in frig or up to a week.

SUMMER MEMORIES *Submitted by Kathy Nash Cary*

I have many evocative food-memories from summer days growing up on my parent's farm in Oldham County. I was pondering these days during the Fourth of July holiday this year, as I returned to the farm and we made our traditional cherry pie. There was a great old sour cherry tree that grew on the farm when my parents moved there in the 1950s and so the cherry pie tradition started a half-century ago. Of course, as all enthusiasts for sour cherries know, you have to be on your toes to get there before the birds have taken their full share. We were lucky, this year, to get six cups of cherries, just enough to make a memorable pie.

We usually kept a cow at the farm, for milking, and she was always called Bessie. I think there may have been Bessie I, Bessie II, Bessie III, and Bessie IV. For this pie my mother treasured the cream that would rise to the top of each bucket of milk.

LONGFIELD FARM CHERRY PIE

For those six cups of cherries, pitted, you add two cups of white sugar and one cup of brown sugar' cook the tart mixture until the fruit and sugars meld; turn it into an unbaked crust and cover with an unbaked top crust' and bake for about 40 minutes at 350 degrees. A wonderful Camille Glenn trick that we always use is to brush the top crust with extra butter—the result being a delicious buttery flakiness covering the sour cherries. Longfield Farm Cherry Pie!

My family also keep a beef cow, for annual slaughter; and of course, there was lots of ground beef in addition to the choicer cuts. I remember that my siblings and I would have to sit and make up beef patties for freezing, and sometimes there would be 500 of them. Needless to say, we enjoyed a lot of meatloaf, too, over the next year. My mother has a delicious moist recipe for the loaf, with the continental twist of having hardboiled eggs in the center. I will share that with you.

HARRODS CREEK SLOW-COOKED MEATLOAF *Submitted by Kathy Cary*

2 lbs. Ground beef
2 eggs, beaten slightly
3 pieces good whole wheat bread, crumbled
2 cups cottage cheese
1 cup yogurt
1 package Lipton onion soup mix

Combine all ingredients lightly, place in a loaf pan, and bake 2 hours at 250 F degrees.

A variation from my early farm days was to hard-boil enough eggs to stretch the length of your loaf pan. When putting in the meat mixture, layer a line of the eggs down the length of the pan after putting in a little less than half the filling; then top with the remainder of the filling. This, I suppose, is a sort of "Oldham County French" touch, and the result is fun to present when sliced.

Among summer fruits, I'll always remember berry picking in the huge raspberry patch. There is a wonderful raspberry pie which I still make today, and which is on the menu at Lilly's during raspberry season—I'll share that with you, too. I remember that we made the pie, always in August, when my aunt would come to visit from Manhattan. It was a pie that easily impressed city-dwellers. Basically, it is a cream cheese filling with lemon zest, in a baked crust; and its crowning glory is a cooked raspberry topping, with the added gilding of fresh raspberries sprinkled on top!

LILLY'S RASPBERRY PIE   *Submitted by Kathy Cary*

Use a cream cheese pie dough for your crust. In a food processor, combine 2½ cups flour, ½ lb. cream cheese, and ½ lb. margarine—not butter this time- with a pinch of salt. Roll out, place in pie pan, weight it, and bake at 350 F degrees for about 25 minutes, or until nicely browned. Set aside.

Cream Cheese Filling
Blend in food processor until smooth, and layer into cooled, cooked pie shell:

    8 oz. cream cheese
    ¼ cup sugar
    1 oz. cream
    1 oz. lemon juice
    1 tsp. grated lemon rind

Glaze
Top cream cheese layer with the following, having cooked the mixture in a heavy saucepan until thickened. Be vigilant—the bottom will scald if you don't watch it carefully. Cool slightly before spreading on the cream cheese layer:

    3 cups fresh or frozen raspberries
    1 cup sugar
    1 tablespoons cornstarch

Before serving, garnish with fresh raspberries

PEWEE VALLEY TEA PARTIES   *These stories and recipes are from Gin Chaudoin.*

One afternoon in the 1940's, the ladies of Pewee Valley Presbyterian Church were invited to "The Beeches" for tea by Mary G. Johnston (we called her Miss Mamie). Miss Mamie was the stepdaughter of Annie Fellows Johnston, the author of The Little Colonel Books. The Beeches had been Miss Annie's home until her death in 1931.

Miss Mamie asked me to serve. As I sat at the table and poured the tea, the maid came to me and asked, "You called"?

"No," I said.

This happened two more times. Each time I assured the maid that I hadn't summoned her. Finally Miss Mamie leaned over to me and said, "Ginny dear, you are touching the bell button on the floor under the dining room table with your foot." Never was I aware that such a thing existed. So—watch were you put your foot!

Having afternoon tea was a daily ritual in several Pewee Valley homes. One hostess was Lillian Fletcher Brackett, who married Charles Brackett, the film producer of "The King and I." Lillian was also the niece of Kate Matthews, who did the photography for the Little Colonel Books. Lillian (we called her Muffy) and her aunt Charlotta Matthews Osborne (or Aunt Lotta as we called her) had tea every day at 4 o'clock for the neighbor ladies in Pewee Valley.

One of the ladies who lived in Pewee Valley read tea leaves. Isabelle Beckley told fortunes through the tea leaves at the Egyptian Tea Room on Third Street in Louisville in the 1930's. It is likely that she also did so at some of the teas that Annie Fellows Johnston gave, because the author was the owner of a special tea-reading cup.

BEATEN BISCUITS

These were served at Kate Matthews' home and Twigmore, the home of Lillian Fletcher Brackett whose husband produced "The King and I".

6 cups sifted flour	Sift dry ingredients then blend in lard. Work on beaten biscuit roller until dough is smooth and satiny and blisters pop (about 20 minutes). Roll to desired thickness. Cut with a 1½" biscuit cutter. Put on baking sheet and prick with a fork 3 times making sure the fork goes all the way through to the pan. Bake at 350 degrees for 30–40 minutes.
1 teaspoon salt	
1 teaspoon baking powder	
3 tablespoons sugar	
1 cup shortening (lard is best)	
1 cup cold milk	

These are some of the favorite recipes served at the teas:

CRÈME DE MENTHE PIE

16 cream cookies, rolled (such as Hydrox)
⅓ cup melted butter
24 large marshmallows
½ cup milk
¼ cup crème de menthe
2 squares semi-sweet chocolate

Crush Hydrox cookies and add to melted butter, press into pan. Melt marshmallows in double boiler, add milk and cool. Add crème de menthe and whipped cream. Pour into shell. Shave chocolate over. Refrigerate 2–3 hours before serving.

PECAN TORTS

Makes 24

1 stick margarine
3 ounces cream cheese
1 cup flour
1 egg
2 tablespoons margarine
¼ cup brown sugar
⅓ cup dark corn syrup
½ cup chopped pecans
½ teaspoon vanilla

Cream together margarine and cream cheese and add flour gradually. Roll into balls and flatten in tort pan. Beat egg and add 2 tablespoons margarine, brown sugar, corn syrup, vanilla and pecans. Dip with spoon into tort pan. Bake at 375 degrees for 20–25 minutes.

PECAN COOKIES

1 cup white sugar
1 cup brown sugar
½ cup shortening
4 eggs
1 cup sifted flour
1 cup chopped pecans
1 teaspoon vanilla

Cream sugar and shortening. Beat eggs one at a time. Add flour, nuts and vanilla. Place on a greased 9 x 13 sheet and bake at 350 degrees for 30 minutes. Sprinkle with powdered sugar when cooled.

SCHOOL DAYS *Submitted by Joyce McKinney*

Mary Clementine Collier was born in northern Oldham County in 1879. She and four siblings grew up on a farm owned by their parents Charles and Catherine Collier. She, one sister and brother never married. Mary, however, struck out on her own in her early twenties.

Mary completed a secretarial course and went to work for the University of Louisville. There she worked most of her professional life. She purchased a home on Hill Street near the University and took in boarders to help defray cost. Each night, she fed boarders their evening meal. Cooking was the love of her life and the young boarding students knew they had struck it rich residing in her home.

She would return to the family farm on Friday evening and stay until Sunday night. Going back to the city she would take fresh farm vegetables and eggs in the spring and fall and lots of canned goods during the winter. During the summer months she helped her sister and brother on the farm.

Bess Collier, Mary Emma Trigg and Mary Clementine Collier circa early 20th century (courtesy of Julia Collier Young).

Students needed snacks and here is one of her favorites and often prepared cookie recipes.

CRUNCH COOKIES

1 cup lightly packed brown sugar
1 tablespoon butter
2 tablespoons flour
1 egg
1 cup nuts (cut up)

Mix flour and sugar and add melted butter. Then add slightly beaten egg and mix well and then add nuts.

Drop on greased cookie sheet and bake in moderate (350F degree oven) for about 10 minutes.

SCHOOL DAY LUNCHES *As told by Ruth Klingenfus*

In the 1920s I remember a lady who would bring a pot of vegetable soup to the school. She gave you a bowl of soup that you took back to your desk. School lunches at that time weren't like they are today. I went to Crestwood School and I usually took a homemade biscuit with a fried egg or a piece of country ham to school. I had a little girlfriend who brought a store-bought bread and bologna sandwich. I thought she was the richest girl in the world. I loved to trade lunches with her.

BREAD PUDDING *Submitted by Ruth Klingenfus*

One of my treasured memories is of coming home from school and finding Mother cooking something good for our supper. She knew how hungry children were and she was happy when she was preparing a good meal for us. This dessert is one I especially remember.

    4 cups milk
    ¾ cup sugar
    4 eggs
    2 cups bread crumbs
    1 tablespoon butter
    ¼ teaspoon salt
    vanilla

Scald milk, stir in sugar and beaten egg yolks, salt and vanilla. Fold in bread crumbs, I prefer biscuits broken into small pieces. Butter the bottom of a two quart casserole dish. Pour batter into pan and place in pan of hot water. Bake for 50 minutes or until firm in a 350 F degree oven. Cover with meringue and bake. Garnish with a little currant jelly or you may like a thin layer of jelly on top of the pudding before the meringue. Serve hot or cold.

Clausen Family Reunion, September 11, 1923: First Row children: Howard Clausen, Elbert Clausen, Oscar "Pat" Leet, Louis Leet, Gertrude "Tootie" Leet, Robert Hoops, Richard Hoops, Bill Hoops, Douglas Shrader, Alberta Shrader, Jack Shrader, Gayler Shrader

Second Row: Dick (R. E. Daddy) Clausen, Helen Clausen on lap, Aunt Minnie Clausen, Marie Leet on lap, Aunt Amelia Clausen Shields, Mary Elizabeth Shields on lap, Aunt Lizzie Clausen Hoops, Grandma Elizabeth Margarett Koenig Clausen, Grandpa John Vincent Clausen, Uncle Fritz (F. H.) Clausen, Aunt Alma "Dolly" Clausen Shrader, Virginia Shrader on lap.

Third Row: Louise "Lula" Ross Clausen, Uncle Jim (J. W.) Leet, John Leet, Elmer Leet, Uncle Herman Hoops, Ed Fellows (husband of Bessie Leet), Aunt Mabel "Sookie" Hensley Clausen, R. "Buddy" Clausen, Uncle Robert "Rob" Shrader

Fourth Row: Fannie Leet, Alma Shields, Katherine Hoops, Margaret Hoops, Bessie Leet Fellows, Elizabeth Clausen, Ella Mae "Sissie" Clausen, Mary "Puddin" Clausen

FAMILY REUNIONS

Family reunions are times when the casseroles, cakes and salads are in abundance. These special events are highlighted by the stories and tales that accompany food and festivities. Sue Conn shares some crowd favorites.

NAN'S OATMEAL CAKE   *Submitted by Sue Conn*

My mother, Nan Coffman, baked this cake recipe for many years. I was not able to visit an Aunt and Uncle without taking an oatmeal cake with me each time. But the funniest thing about this recipe had to be when my father-in-law, Frank Conn, found out the cake's name. He had been a cook in the Army and had to prepare and serve large quantities of oatmeal. He swore that he would never eat oatmeal again. Then one day when asking, who would like a slice of Oatmeal cake, he discovered the name. From that date forward he never ate my Oatmeal Cake even though he had enjoyed it previously for many years.

Oatmeal Cake

    1 cup uncooked oatmeal soaked in
        1⅓ cups of boiling water for 20 minutes
    1 cup sugar
    1 cup brown sugar, firmly packed
    1 cup margarine melted
    2 eggs, lightly beaten
    1⅓ cup flour
    1 teaspoon vanilla
    1 teaspoon baking soda
    1 teaspoon baking powder
    1½ teaspoons cinnamon
    ½ teaspoon salt

In a large bowl, mix sugars together with margarine. Add eggs and beat after each addition. Sift together dry ingredients and then mix dry ingredients into cream mixture, and add vanilla. Then add oatmeal to the cream mixture.

Grease and flour a glass oven dish, 12 x 7½ x 1¾, (need to use this size pan, otherwise larger pan dries cake out and makes too thin). Bake at 325 F degrees for approx. 35 minutes. Cool cake 10 minutes before frosting.

Coconut Frosting

    1 cup brown sugar, firmly packed
    1 tablespoon butter or margarine
    1 cup shredded coconut
    ⅓ cup evaporated milk
    ½ cup chopped pecans.

Cream sugar and margarine together. Fold in coconuts and nuts. Moisten with the evaporated milk. Spread over top of cake. Put in broiler for a few minutes until the frosting is bubbly and oozes over the top of cake—will set up once removed from oven.

CHICKEN AND DRESSING CASSEROLE *Submitted by Sue Conn*

4 cups chicken, baked and chopped
2 cups chicken broth, canned or from baking
1 stick of butter or margarine, melted
1 pkg. Pepperidge Farm Corn Bread Stuffing
1 teaspoon ground sage
1 can cream of chicken soup
1 can cream of celery soup
8 ounces sour cream

In bowl add melted margarine, stuffing and sage mixing thoroughly. Sprinkle one third stuffing in bottom of 9 x 13 casserole dish. Layer with chopped chicken. Mix together soups and sour cream. Spread evenly over chicken. Top with remaining stuffing. Pour chicken broth over casserole. Let stand 2 hours or overnight in refrigerator. Bake at 325 F degrees for 35–45 minutes. If taking from refrigerator overnight allow to sit out at room temperature for approximately 30 minutes.

SLAW EVERLASTING *Submitted by Sue Conn*

4 pounds cabbage, shredded (2 large heads)
2 carrots, grated
1 green pepper, chopped
1 medium onion, chopped
5 ribs celery, chopped

Dressing

1½ cups sugar
1 cup vinegar
1 teaspoon pepper
1 teaspoon salt
1 teaspoon celery seed
1 tablespoon Knox gelatin
¼ cup water
1 cup vegetable oil

Mix vegetable in large bowl and set aside while preparing dressing.

Heat sugar and vinegar until sugar dissolves. Cool slightly and add salt, pepper and celery seed. Dissolve gelatin in water and add to the sugar/vinegar mix. Cool in refrigerator until consistency of cream, then add vegetable oil, beat with electric mixer and pour over vegetables. Let stand in refrigerator 24 hours before serving. Keeps for a week.

Lucy Trigg made this big dish often for reunions, church functions, etc. as did Letty Mount.

CHICKEN SOUFFLÉ

Cook a whole chicken (5 lbs or more) until it starts to fall off the bone. Take 1 loaf of stale bread broken in small pieces and then pour 1 quart chicken stock over bread. Let stand 1 hour. Beat 5 eggs into 1 quart of milk. Cut chicken into small bits and add to bread mixture. Add milk to this and mix lightly; season with salt and pepper. Bake in flat well greased pan at 350 F degrees until it sets. Serve with mushroom sauce or other white sauce. Serves 15–20 folks.

RUTH DEIBEL'S GERMAN POTATO SALAD *Submitted by Mrs. Tom Deibel*

I started dating Tom Deibel in 1963. The first time he took me to meet his family was his mother's family reunion held every 4th of July on their farm near Crestwood. One of the dishes I was introduced to that day was German potato salad. There were at least 2 or 3 different family recipes at each picnic. Everyone put their own little twist to their recipe. After Tom and I married, I asked his mother to share the recipe with me. She didn't have a recipe. The next time she made it she measured and wrote down what she used. The recipe she came up with is the best I've ever had. It is as follows:

6 medium potatoes
3 pieces bacon
2 tablespoons flour
1 tablespoon salt
¾ cup sugar
¾ cup vinegar
½ cup water
¼ cup chopped onion
¼ cup chopped celery

Slice boiled potatoes. Fry bacon, remove bacon and drain. In bacon grease add flour, sugar, vinegar, salt, and water. Mix well and bring to a boil. Add celery and onions and simmer for about 20 minutes. Pour mixture over potatoes. Can be refrigerated for several days. Let sit out a couple of hours before serving, should be room temperature.

THANKSGIVING DAY

Persimmon Pudding *Submitted by Elizabeth Cull and Jeanne Gibson*

Many years ago, my Mother and Father would patiently wait for fall to arrive, which meant persimmons would be ripe. They always gathered containers and piled into their old Ford for the long journey all the way to Crestwood in Oldham County. They knew of a big old persimmon tree by the railroad tracks and the bank, where they could pick up plump, juicy persimmons. They carefully avoided all of the honeybees and gathered as many persimmons as they could, as their mouths watered in anticipation of the tasty cookies and pudding that were to come.

At home they would patiently rub the fruit with a big wooden spoon, pushing the pulp thru a colander. It took quite a few to produce a cup of golden pulp. Usually they froze the pulp in one-cup portions in cottage cheese cartons for Thanksgiving and Christmas. This was a time before zip bags and plastic containers were available in stores.

On Thanksgiving Day, the wonderful aroma of spices, sugar and persimmons would permeate the house as the persimmon pudding baked in the oven. Late in the day, we'd enjoy warm pudding with fresh whipped cream—the finale of a delicious turkey dinner with all the trimmings.

This tradition continues until this day, although the family has scattered to California, Maryland, Texas, North Carolina, Georgia and Arkansas. We always keep an eye out for persimmon trees as we visit friends and travel in the fall; it's always a thrill when we discover one.

PERSIMMON PUDDING

1 pint persimmon pulp
1 pint milk
2 eggs, separated
½ cup sugar
4 tablespoons melted butter
2 cups all purpose flour
½ teaspoon cinnamon
½ teaspoon nutmeg
½ teaspoon salt
½ teaspoon soda
1 rounded teaspoon baking powder

Mix egg yolks, sugar and pulp together. In another bowl, sift flour, soda, baking powder, salt, cinnamon and nutmeg together. Beat egg whites until stiff. Add milk and flour mixture alternately to pulp mixture. Add melted butter and then fold in beaten egg whites. Pour into a greased 1½ quart casserole and bake 1 hour in a 325 F degree oven. Test with a toothpick until it comes out clean. As soon as the pudding comes from the oven, spoon immediately into a large bowl. Serve with whipped cream or orange sauce.

AMBER PIE *Submitted by Cindy Jeffries Barr*

This recipe came from my great-grandmother Sally Bett Smiser who was married to Hubbard Buckner Goodrich. They had a farm in Ballardsville. Sally wrote a social column for the Oldham Era from around the turn of the century up until the 1940s, when she passed away. This recipe is a family favorite that has been passed down. The name comes from the color of the pie. Because it is so rich and full of delicious calories, we now serve it as a special treat only twice a year, at Thanksgiving and at Christmas

2 eggs, beaten
1 cup sugar
½ cup sweet cream
½ cup butter
1 cup blackberry jam
1 tablespoon pure vanilla extract
2 tablespoons cornstarch dissolved
    in a little bit of water

Combine first 6 ingredients in a saucepan on top of the stove. Once this mixture is warm, slowly stir in cornstarch. Cook over medium heat until thick-do not boil. This can take 15 minutes or more. Pour into a baked pie crust and refrigerate.

FUNERAL FOODS

Peak's Funeral Home, Radcliffe Funeral Home and Stoess Funeral Home were the three places in Oldham County during the Twentieth Century where family and friends came together to share stories and food around the memories of their loved ones. People became known for the dishes and cakes that were brought to the funerals. Peak's funeral home employed women and African Americans very early on in the Twentieth Century and boasted to have the first automobile hearse in Oldham County. Both Richard Radcliffe and Milton Carl Stoess, gave many volunteer hours to ensure that local cemeteries were maintained and respected. Jean Kay Radcliffe and Lucy Ricketts, Jean's daughter, shared some of these favorites recipes.

Peak's Funeral Home

G. W. PEAK & SON

Funeral Directors For
Nearly Thirty Years

17 Years In LaGrange

First Automobile Hearse In Oldham County
First and Only Limousine Type Funeral
Car In Oldham County
First and Only Funeral Home In the County
First and Only Funeral Directors In This County
to Furnish a Lady Assistant

Advertisement for Peak's Funeral Home (Oldham County Historical Society Collection).

Radcliffe Family circa 1954, left to right: Linda Kaye Radcliffe, Jean Kay Radcliffe, Lucy Radcliffe, Richard Radcliffe (courtesy Lucy Radcliffe Ricketts)

BROCCOLI CASSEROLE

2 pkgs frozen,
    chopped broccoli
½ cup finely chopped onion
6 tablespoons butter or
margarine
2 tablespoons flour

Sauce
½ cup water
1 cup grated American cheese
3 eggs well-beaten
½ cup cracker or bread crumbs

Cook and drain broccoli. Saute onion in four tablespoons butter until soft. Stir in flour. Add water and cook over low heat until mixture thickens and comes to a boil. Blend in cheese. Combine sauce and broccoli, add eggs, and mix gently. Cover casserole with crumbs, dot with remaining two tablespoons of butter, and bake in oven at 325 F degrees for 30 minutes. Serves 8.

CHILI CHEESE BALL

1 lb. American Cheese
1 small 3-ounce pkg. cream cheese
1 clove smashed garlic
1 cup pecans
1 can of hot chili powder

Grind American cheese, garlic and pecans together. Add and mix softened cream cheese into mixture. Form into large round ball. Put a generous amount of chili powder on wax paper and roll cheese ball around in it. Refrigerate 24 hours.

GARLIC GRITS

1 cup quick grits
6 ounces Kraft garlic cheese
1 stick margarine or butter
2 eggs and milk

Cook grits as directed on box. While hot, add garlic cheese and margarine. Stir until melted. Cool. Break 2 eggs in a cup and add enough milk to equal 1 cup. Beat well. Add grits, stir and pour into buttered dish. Sprinkle with cracker crumbs. Bake at 350 F degrees for 45 minutes.

3 large onions, chopped
3 cloves garlic, minced
3 tablespoons olive oil
2 pounds ground top sirloin
1 large can tomato sauce
1 small can tomato paste
½ cup water
1 teaspoon oregano
1 teaspoon sugar
1 cup red wine
2 bay leaves
Pepper to taste
Salt to taste

1 pound flat lasagna pasta
1½ pounds ricotta cheese
1 pound mozzarella cheese, coarsely grated

Brown onions and garlic in olive oil. Add meats and cook until gray. Add all other ingredients except cheese and pasta and simmer slowly for 3 hours in a heavy pot tightly covered. Boil pasta according to package directions and wash with cold water to remove excess starch. In large greased pan (preferably long, deep, and rectangular) place alternate layers of pasta, meat, sauce, and cheeses. Start with a pasta layer, end with cheeses. Bake at 325 F for about 1 hour or until bubbly.

WORLD WAR II

World War II Special Caramels

Rachel Waters told her daughter, Lucy Waters Clausen, that she found and began using this caramel recipe during World War II. The caramels were recommended for soldiers' care packages since they traveled and kept well. After the war, Mother made multiple batches between Thanksgiving and Christmas to give as gifts. Our basement was full of tins of all sizes for the gifting. A person who received a whole batch knew he rated high. My grandfather was one of those people—he ate his caramels one a day and never shared.

Each caramel is wrapped individually like a mini-package. Mother always said that was the hardest part, so she had Daddy do it.

RACHEL'S CARAMELS

In a large, heavy pan, combine:
  2 cups white sugar
  2 cups white karo syrup

Boil the above until clear and bubbly. Add 1 stick of oleo margarine. Allow that to melt and mixture to cook well for a while. Slowly add a 12 ounce can of evaporated milk. Cook to desired hard ball stage. Remove from heat. Add 1 teaspoon of vanilla and ¾ cup of pecans. Pour into a well-greased 9 square pan. Cool, cut and wrap.

BOURBON PRALINES

Submitted by Lucy Waters Clausen

Rachel Waters and Ruth Williamson had a holiday tradition of candy making. These pralines were always made at the Williamson house. The process is ticklish and success was celebrated with a highball.

2 cups sugar (granulated)
1 teaspoon baking soda
Pinch of salt
1 cup buttermilk
2 tablespoons butter or margarine
2⅓ cup pecans
2½ ounces of bourbon
Candy thermometer

Right to left: Lucy Waters Clausen, seated, Rachel Waters and Ruth Williamson toasting to successful candy making efforts, circa 1960s; baby is Louise Clausen. (courtesy of Lucy Waters Clausen).

In a large saucepan combine the first four ingredients. Cook for 5 minutes or until mixture reaches 210 degrees over high heat. Stir often and scrape bottom of the pan. Add butter and pecans. Cook and stir constantly until mixture reaches 230 degrees. Remove from heat. Add bourbon and let cool for about 1 minute. Beat by hand about 5 minutes. Drop by tablespoon onto wax paper and allow to harden. Makes about 2 dozen.

CHRISTMAS HOMEMADE EGGNOG *Submitted by Sharon Clark*

This is a recipe that has been in my family for as many years as I can remember. On every Christmas morning we would get up and open our gifts. Then as soon as the gifts were all open, my Dad would go into the kitchen and start the eggnog. It was almost a ritual at my house. We would all stand around and watch him make it, then when it was all complete, Momma would get out her antique punch bowl and cups and we would all have a glass of eggnog together. If company came Daddy would always make another bowl and everyone would have another cup!

6 eggs
1½ cups confectioner sugar
1 quart whole milk
1 quart half and half
1 pint whipping cream
1 teaspoon vanilla extract
1 cup bourbon or whiskey
Nutmeg

Separate eggs and set whites aside. In large mixing bowl, mix 6 egg yolks and 1 cup of sugar together

well. Then add milk, half and half, whipping cream and mix all together well. Add the vanilla while mixing, then add the bourbon. Pour mixture in punch bowl.

Beat egg whites until fluffy. Then add the rest of the sugar while beating. Spoon the egg whites on top of the eggnog and sprinkle with nutmeg. (Editor's note: this recipe calls for raw eggs which can be a source of salmonella bacteria).

SHRIMP CHRISTMAS TREE *Submitted by Linda Roberts*

1 12-in. Styrofoam cone
12–15 cherry tomatoes
2 small heads curly endive lettuce
3 lbs large shrimp (cooked, peeled,
    deveined and chilled)

Starting at the bottom of the cone working upwards, attach greens to cone with toothpicks.

Attach cherry tomatoes in cone with toothpicks for tree decorations. Fill tree with shrimp using colored toothpicks. Arrange remaining shrimp around base of tree.

Refrigerate until serving time. Tree can be prepared up to 3 hours ahead of serving.

COTTAGE CHEESE RING AND AUNT MELVINA'S DRESSING
Submitted by Linda Pollard Roberts

This recipe has been prepared by my mother as a staple item of every holiday family gathering since I can remember. No matter what the menu, this is a dish that is requested by all the family members.

Cottage Cheese Ring

1 envelope gelatin
¼ cup water
2 cups cottage cheese
12 chopped olives
¼ cup chopped nuts
1 teaspoon chopped green pepper
1 teaspoon chopped onion
¼ cup chopped pimento

Dissolve gelatin in water and add the remaining ingredients. Press into ring mold greased with mayonnaise. Serve with the following dressing:

Aunt Melvina's Dressing

1 cup sugar
½ cup vinegar
2 teaspoons dry mustard
2 teaspoons celery seed
2 teaspoons paprika
2 teaspoons salt
4 tablespoons chopped onion
2 cups salad oil—cold

Mix all ingredients, adding the oil last and slowly. Serve in a gravy bowl and pour over the cottage cheese ring when served.

NANA CULL'S PERSIMMON COOKIES *Submitted by Jeanne Gibson*

My mother always made dozens and dozens of these and gave them to friends and family for Christmas. They were such a delicacy and were savored by all. They knew what was in the cellophane package tied with the bright red bow when Mother came carrying them. It wouldn't be Christmas at our house without a batch of persimmon cookies to enjoy and leave a few on a plate for Santa.

½ cup butter
1 cup sugar
1 large egg
1 cup persimmon pulp (can be
    purchased at specialty food stores)
2 cups all purpose flour
½ teaspoon cinnamon
½ teaspoon nutmeg
1 teaspoon soda
1 cup chopped nuts
1 cup chopped raisins or dates

Cream together the butter and sugar. Dissolve soda in pulp. Add egg and pulp to creamed mixture. Mix dry ingredients adding nuts and raisins. Mix dry ingredients with creamed mixture. Drop by teaspoons on greased cookie sheet. Bake at 350 F degrees about 15 minutes or until firm. A dollop of butter-orange juice-powdered sugar icing on top of each cookie after baking adds zip!

CHARLOTTE RUSSE *Submitted by John Plymale*

On Christmas Day my grandmother always prepared her special dish of Charlotte Russe. One Christmas my grandmother and my brother were sitting together after dinner awaiting the traditional dessert. When I was helping clean up from dinner and serve dessert, I saw a pound of butter and noticed it was the same color as the "Russe" custard. I formed ladyfingers around the butter, topped it with a cherry and served that to my brother and the Charlotte Russe to my grandmother. They both took large bites. My grandmother asked, "Isn't this wonderful?" All my brother could do was smile and nod his head, and then give me a dirty look!

1 level tablespoon gelatin dissolved
    in ¼ cup water
5 tablespoons powdered sugar
½ teaspoon vanilla
Pinch of salt
3 large eggs, separated
1 pint whipping cream
1 package lady fingers

Line a glass bowl or individual glass dishes with ladyfingers. Dissolve gelatin in cold water in a small custard dish and set in warm water to melt. Beat egg whites stiff. Beat whipping cream. Beat egg yolks well and add salt, vanilla, sugar and gelatin. Fold in beaten egg whites and half of the whipped cream. Pour custard like filling into bowl or dishes. Top with remaining whipped cream. Garnish with a cherry. (Editor's note: this recipe calls for raw eggs which can be sources of salmonella bacteria).

CHRISTMAS COOKIES *Submitted by Sara Deibel*

These are recipes from my grandmother that we baked for Christmas. They are rather involved and require time and work, but they are well worth the effort.

My mother, sister, and I would set aside a week to bake for Christmas. We always used my grandmother's rolling pin, wood rolling board, and large stoneware mixing crocks. My mother taught my sister and me to make these recipes. It really helps to see them being made in person because they can be a little tricky. My mother would never use anything but Tupelo honey in the strudel, so we would travel south every summer until we could find it. Really, I think it was just a good excuse to take a trip! My grandmother always made her own powdered sugar. She died in 1942, three years before I was born.

NUT STRUDEL

Filling:
- 1½ lbs. ground pecans
- ½ lb. ground English walnuts
- 4 cups sugar
- ½ cup (Tupelo) honey (You can only found Tupelo in the south; another high grade honey will work)
- ½ teaspoon vanilla
- 3 cups milk

Dough:
- ½ lb. slated butter (at room temperature)
- 1 cup egg yolks
- 1 pint cream or half and half plus
    - 2 cakes of yeast
- 2 tablespoons of sugar
- 1 teaspoon vanilla
- 6 cups flour

Cream butter. Add yolks and mix well. Heat cream and sugar until luke warm then crumble yeast in milk and let stand just a little. Add vanilla, milk, and flour to butter, and then add eggs a little at a time until the dough is soft and sticky. Place dough in a greased (Crisco) cloth and tie end. Place in a very large mixing crock (if you have one) filled

with cold water and let stand for 1½ to two hours until dough floats to the top.

Place dough on a floured rolling board and knead a few times. (Don't overwork the dough). Cut into 6 equal parts and cover with a dry cloth. Roll out one part at a time into a rectangle and spread with part of the filling to the edge. Then roll up into one long roll. Place on a greased baking sheet with the seam down (you can place three rolls on one baking sheet so save room). Continue the same process with the other 5 pieces of dough. Place pans in a warm place and cover with a wet rag for 1 to 1½ hours and let rolls rise.

Topping:
Mix together ¼ cup sugar and ¾ cup chopped nuts.

Beat 1 whole egg with 1 tablespoon of water and brush over the rolls. Then sprinkle with the sugar and nut mixture. Bake at 325 degrees for 35–40 minutes. Cool and store.

To serve, cut into thin slices.

KIPFEL

½ lb unsalted butter
8 eggs (separated)
2 cups flour
1 cup sugar
2 cups English walnuts (ground finely)
½ teaspoon vanilla

Cream butter, work in 8 eggs yolks (unbeaten) and then add flour. Refrigerate for 4–6 hours. Roll into small balls. (I use the small side of a melon baller)

Beat 8 egg whites until stiff. Carefully fold in sugar, nuts, and vanilla.

On a lightly floured rolling board, roll out balls into VERY thin rounds. Layer the rounds with the egg white mixture (not too thick) and roll up into tubes, then shape into crescents. Place on ungreased cookie sheet and bake for about 10 minutes at 325 degrees; or until golden brown.

While cookies are still warm, sprinkle with powdered sugar. Cool and store. These cookies are very time consuming, but well worth the effort! They will melt in your mouth!

My grandmother's rolling board is about 200 years old, if you do not have a wood board, I would suggest using a clean counter top.

SPRINGLES   *Submitted by Elizabeth Fendley*

Two or three weeks before Christmas, Momma would start baking. She always made Springles and other cookies. On Christmas Eve, she would make a crock of eggnog with fresh eggs and fresh milk. Grandma and Grandpa Clausen, along with whoever else was at home, would come over for refreshments. Then Santa Claus would come (who was played by Uncle Dick Clausen until he was married, and then by my Dad). After Santa Claus visited, Momma would pass out Springles to eat, and we would enjoy them all through the holiday.

4 eggs
1 lb sifted confectioner's sugar
Grated rind of one lemon
4½ cup of sifted flour, a little more
      may be needed
1 teaspoon baking powder
¼ teaspoon salt
1 teaspoon (scant) anise oil
1 tablespoon honey

Beat eggs until light in color and then add the honey, lemon rind, and anise. Sift flour, sugar, baking powder, and salt together. Sift over wet ingredients, adding about ¼ of the dry mixture at a time and mixing well after each addition. Dough will be very stiff.

Roll out about ¼ of the mixture at a time with a plain rolling pin to about ¼" in thickness. Flour a Springles rolling pin well and roll over dough to get a clear-cut design. Cut with a sharp knife, put on table or counter and let stand 12 hours uncovered or over night. Bake on a greased cookie sheet in a moderate 250 degree oven for 15 minutes or until light brown. Store Springles in an airtight container for at least two weeks to allow the flavor to develop.

Favorite Places to Eat and Visit

Oldham County has had its memorable share of wonderful places to go and eat. Many of these establishments were located along Highway 42 which was the main road from Louisville to Cincinnati before I-71 opened in 1970. Several other restaurants and inns were located in towns along the railroad tracks. Today we have some new restaurants that are adding their own unique flavor and culture to the community.

GOSHEN GARDENS

Submitted by Annice Johnson this article was written by Annice's mother, Helen Belknap Tupper. Helen's family owned Land O'Goshen farm on Hwy. 42 and built Goshen Gardens restaurant on the front of the property to tempt travelers driving between Louisville and Cincinnati. Goshen Gardens served customers for many years; since its closing it has played host to the local Lion's Club and many community events.

As written by Mrs. Tupper:

I can't remember the exact date when Goshen Gardens was built. I know it was in the early 30's when the Big Depression was in full swing. The stone was quarried off Land O'Goshen on south Buckeye Lane as was the stone for the new wing of our house on the farm. Local labor was used and I believe the mason was Mr. Guyton. The brick floors were done with paving bricks from Louisville streets, hence the shiny polished surface. The beams in the main room came from an old smoke house, and when the building was closed up for a few days it smelled like bacon and ham. The original plan, which included the smaller building next door, called for an excellent restaurant and a country market for meat and produce—all local. There were also gas pumps in front of the market.

I don't know who the early chefs were, but they were mostly unsuccessful, either from lack of ability or excessive drinking. How Daddy (Mr. William Belknap) found Mr. Willy Lanfer, I don't know but he was the right man for the job. He had trained under the famous

Goshen Gardens photo (courtesy of The Oldham Era)

Mr. Solger, who catered to society up and down the Mississippi. Mr. Willy promptly pointed out that serving only Land O'Goshen beef wouldn't work since the "non-steak" parts would overwhelm the restaurant cooler. So, Mr. Willy ordered most of the meat from town, and it was always good. I know this because I regularly rode my pony through the fields (too dangerous near Hwy. 42 because of all the trucks and cars speeding towards Cincinnati) and Mr. Willy would cook a steak for me as I watched from a stool in the kitchen. He said people were wrong not to salt meat before cooking it. He was known to be stingy, but he was always very generous to me.

The most famous of his offerings was his salad dressing. It was a hot creamy Italian type which Daddy and I found too spicy and hot but everyone else wanted the recipe. The recipe was a closely guarded secret: Mr. Willy's niece worked for him as a hostess and bookkeeper and she tried to learn it. However, Mr. Willy always managed to send her on an errand at the crucial moment and when she returned the dressing was made and sitting in the icebox. Mr. Willy had promised the recipe to Daddy before he died. Unfortunately, when Mr. Willy summoned Daddy to his deathbed, Daddy was out-of-town and so the recipe died with Mr. Willy.

Mr. Willy was a terrible social snob, probably left over from his days with Mr. Solger; catering weddings and luncheons for society. Daddy would stop by his restaurant and ask Mr. Willy how business was. "Wonderful, wonderful, Mr. William! Mrs. Woozit and three ladies (were here)". It didn't matter that they were the only customers—they were the right sort! There were four stools at the counter where one could be served a quick lunch. The hamburgers were excellent and appealed to the trucking trade who knew about them. When the truckers would stop and eat at the counter, Mr. Willy would refer to them as a "pitiful trade, pitiful trade".

The menu was good but limited—steak, chicken, lamb chops and occasionally fish. This was before the advent of frozen food, so seafood was a little suspect. In fact, the food was good enough to merit several A's from the Duncan Hines travel guide.

When World War II started, it rang the death knell for Goshen Gardens. With gas rationing, patrons hadn't enough to drive to the country, nor did the waiters. In addition, Mr. Willy's legs and feet were bad from all the standing on concrete and brick floors, especially since he was none to slim. And so, Goshen Gardens closed.

As I said, I rode my pony everywhere. I didn't have or want a bicycle. I went by pony to see Mr. Willy and to my other favorite place for goodies. It was right at the gate to Land O'Goshen—the home of Mr. Alan Adams, the farm manager. A lifelong bachelor, his housekeeper was his spinster sister, Miss Agnes Adams—Miss Aggie (they were cousins of Colonel Harlan Sanders). Their figures attested to her cooking. My brother Burke was lucky enough to board with them when my brother Jonathan and I had whooping cough. He bragged about all the wonderful breakfasts, pork chops and such. What I loved best was her fondant, the likes of which I have never tasted since. She tried to teach me to make it and I don't think she held back any secrets, but I never could duplicate it. Looking back I see that my pony spent a lot of time tied to fences while I enjoyed all these treats. She never once broke loose leaving me to walk home: a very good pony!

THE MELROSE INN *Submitted by Ann Smiser*

In 1960, Jack and Ann Smiser bought the Melrose Inn from Robert and Genevieve Barrickman. Previously this was a residential home to many families dating back to 1878. At that time there was a broad road that extended from Prospect in Jefferson County to several hundred feet in Oldham County. The toll station was located across the road from the house and it cost a nickel to travel it for a half a mile. According to the court house records in LaGrange, people by the name of Demeler owned the property. In 1906, the Doretha family bought the property and in 1946 it was purchased by a Williams family from Louisville. They sold it to the Van Horns and in the same year the Van Horns sold it to Joe Larrabee. In 1949 the Barrickmans acquired the house and five acres of land and made it their home.

In 1951, after Jack and Ann Smiser built the Melrose Motel, The Barrickman's decided to convert their house into a restaurant, which they named Melrose Inn. After operating it for 11 years, and in the same time frame, leasing it to the Walter Kern family, they decided in 1960 to sell it to Jack and Ann Smiser. The Kern family brought the recipe for Derby Pie from Virginia and it was an instant success. So much so, they got a patent, and for a number of years the Melrose Inn was the only place you could buy it. The Kern family leased the restaurant from the Barrickmans and then the Smisers for several years, but due to poor health, the Smisers started operating the restaurant in 1961.

The Inn enjoyed success with its good home cooked food, reasonable prices, and served breakfast, lunch, and dinner 7 days a week from 1961 to 1977. At that time the motel and inn were sold to other owners.

The following are a few of the popular dishes that were served:

MELROSE INN DRESSING

One of our most popular salads was the Kentucky Bibb lettuce with the Melrose Inn dressing!

   1 cup vinegar
   1 cup half and half
   1 tablespoon butter
   1 tablespoon ground mustard
   1 teaspoon celery seed
   1 cup sugar
   1 teaspoon salt
   ½ teaspoon flour
   4 eggs beaten

Put butter and vinegar together. Cook until it comes to a boil and add cream, mustard, salt, sugar, flour, and eggs. Cook until thick, whisking continuously. Arrange Bibb lettuce leaves in individual salad bowls and put the dressing in the middle.

CHOCOLATE CHIP AND ENGLISH WALNUT PIE

At the present time, this pie is being made in the Bluegrass Industrial Park in Louisville, KY. It can be purchased in a number of stores in several different states.

Mix one half cup of flour with one cup of sugar and add two, slightly beaten eggs; then add one stick of melted butter that has had a chance to cool. Fold in one cup of broken English walnuts, one cup of chocolate chips, and one teaspoon of vanilla. Pour into an unbaked pie shell and bake in a 350 degree oven for 30 minutes. It should not be runny, but thick and chewy. Serve warm with whipped cream or vanilla ice cream.

MELROSE INN BISCUITS

Customers could not get enough of our biscuits for breakfast. For sixteen years the same cooks, Bessie Kelley and her daughter, Gerry, made the biscuits without a specific recipe; however the following one is as close as it gets to the real thing!

2 cups of Our Best Self Rising Flour
    (milled in Smithfield, KY)
3 rounded tablespoons of T. Fischer's lard
¼ cup of whole sweet milk

Gently mix these ingredients, roll out on a floured board to ¼" thickness. Cut with a 2" biscuit cutter and bake at 450 for 15 minutes.

CREAMED SPINACH

1 10 ounce box of frozen chopped spinach
1 small onion chopped fine
Cook this together with one teaspoon salt
    for 5 minutes.

Remove from heat and add 3 ounces of cream cheese, 1 tablespoon butter, 1 tablespoon flour, and ½ cup half and half. This can be put in a casserole and kept hot in the oven or served from the cooking pan. Sprinkle a bit of nutmeg on top.

CHICKEN TRAIL INN *Submitted by Chris and Diedre Gibson*

Ruth Heyser was a long standing resident of Oldham County and was very active in her community and church. She volunteered at the hospital and served on the Cooperative Extension Board. She was a member of the Honorable Order of Kentucky Colonels in 1971 and helped organize the crossroads Homemakers Club. She also supported and served for many senior citizens in LaGrange and Oldham County, Kentucky. Ruth also

Ruth and Ted Heyser, Chicken Trail Inn Owners (courtesy of Chris and Diedre Gibson)

Chicken Trail Inn Menu Cover (Oldham County History Center Collection).

owned a business for several years and taught at Chicken Trail Ceramics. Ruth was well known for her cooking and honored in April 1988 with a 1st place win from the American Dairy Association. She was also second place winner that same year in the Dairylicious Pasta Recipe Contest, with her pasta recipe, Noodles Southern Style. She will always be remembered for her Barbecue Meatballs at large family gatherings.

Ted Heyser was a native of Leitchfield, Kentucky. Ted graduated from Jefferson School of Law and was a practicing attorney in Louisville for several years. In 1938, he purchased a farm at Prospect and began the well-known "Chicken Trail Inn Restaurant" which he owned and operated until his retirement in 1969. He was also a great lover of thoroughbred horses, which he bred, raised and raced.

CHICKEN TRAIL ROQUEFORT CHEESE DRESSING

(makes one gallon)
- 1¾ pound Treasure Cave brand Blue Cheese (cut in small chunks)
- 10 drops Tabasco sauce
- 10 drops of garlic juice
- 1 tablespoon of Worcestershire Sauce
- 1 pint buttermilk
- Hoffman House Mayonnaise

Stir gently, until thoroughly mixed. DO NOT BEAT. Leave real lumpy. Add about one pint of buttermilk. Stir gently. Then add enough Hoffman House mayonnaise to make the gallon full. Fold in GENTLY until mixed. DO NOT BEAT.

This dressing is better refrigerated three or four days before using.

RUTH HEYSER'S MEATBALLS AND BARBEQUE SAUCE

Meatballs
- 2 pounds ground beef
- 1 can (12 oz) evaporated milk
- 1 cup old-fashioned oatmeal
- 1 cup cracker crumbs
- 2 eggs
- ½ cup chopped onion
- ½ teaspoon garlic powder
- 2 teaspoons salt
- 2 teaspoons chili powder

Mix all ingredients together. Shape into walnut-size meatballs. (can be frozen).

Sauce
- 2 cups catsup
- 1 cup brown sugar
- ½ teaspoon liquid smoke
- ½ teaspoon garlic powder
- ¼ cup chopped onion
- Mix sauce together (can be frozen)

When ready to cook: Mix meatballs and sauce together in a roaster. Cook in 350 F degree oven for 45–60 minutes. Makes approx. 66 meatballs.

THE ASHBOURNE INN

The Ashbourne Inn still stands at the crossroads of Sligo Road and Hwy. 42. The Inn, owned by Mr. and Mrs. Lyons Brown, featured home cooked dishes and the beautiful limestone structure was a favorite for locals and visitors.

Walter Beaumont serving at Ashbourne Inn circa 1960s (courtesy of Ida Beaumont).

ASHBOURNE INN CHICKEN CACCIATORE

(6 to 8 servings)

4 lb. hen
Flour to dredge chicken
Butter to brown chicken (1/4 cup)

Disjoint chicken. Sprinkle generously with salt and pepper and dredge pieces in flour. Melt butter in a dutch oven and brown chicken. Cover with the following sauce and cook slowly until chicken is tender.

Sauce

¼ cup butter
1 tablespoon finely minced onion
1 carrot, cut in cubes
1 turnip, cut in cubes
¼ cup flour
1 cup white wine
1 teaspoon salt
⅛ teaspoon black pepper

Cayenne pepper
2 cups stewed strained tomatoes
1 cup boiling water
1 clove garlic
1 cup sliced mushrooms sautéed 5 minutes in 1 tablespoon butter (to be added 10 minutes before chicken is done)

Pour off fat from the pan after the chicken is browned and add enough butter to make ¼ cup. Add flour, salt, pepper and cayenne and stir in skillet until flour is browned. Add tomatoes gradually and cook 5 minutes, then strain over chicken. Add all other ingredients, except sautéed mushrooms. Put the top on the pan and simmer slowly until chicken seems very tender when stuck with a fork—1 to 2 hours. Ten minutes before removing from stove add the sautéed mushrooms. If mixture cooks too thick, add more water and wine mixed in equal proportions. Serve with Spanish or Yellow Rice.

Favorite Places to Eat and Visit

PETE'S POOL HALL *Located on Main Street in LaGrange*

Recollections of Jim King, transcribed by Ellen Perkins

Between college and teaching in Greensboro, North Carolina, Jim King worked as a mail carrier. Pete's was his normal hangout, so each morning he stopped by for apple pie with ice cream. The most expensive item on the menu was the Pete Burger that cost 45 cents. According to Mr. King, this consisted of two hamburger patties, dressed, with cheese and some kind of mayonnaise sauce. Jim King was down at Pete's when his parents at home took the phone call offering him a teaching job in Greensboro, NC. Though he missed the call, he took the job, and there he met his wife.

Hugh Martin sitting on stool at Pete's Pool Hall circa 1960s (Oldham County History Center Abney Collection)

PETE BURGER FROM PETE'S POOL HALL

Submitted by Doris Ingram, Pete's daughter

My dad felt he could make his own special burger as good as any other burger, which he did, and he named it Pete's Burger. Divide about ⅓ lb hamburger into two burgers and cook fresh when ordered. Toast the hamburger bun on the grill as the burgers cook. Dress the bun with the special dressing recipe that only my dad knew. Layer with lettuce, tomatoes, first burger, a slice of cheese, the second burger and pickles. The price was 45 cents.

Pete's Pool Hall opened c. 1953 on Main Street in LaGrange. My dad cooked the burgers and prepared sandwiches for customers. My mother, a school teacher, would cook chili at home and take it to the pool room. Available also for sale were the usual french fries, potato chips, candy and other snacks. Around 1960, my father realized that only males were coming to play pool. He thought women would enjoy playing pool too, so he started offering classes to teach females to play. The women would come for classes, and we would feed them lunch. The women who learned to play would then play against each other.

MARY D. SHOPPE   *Proprietor: Mary D. Thompson   Submitted by Peggy Burge*

The Mary D. Shoppe was a popular hang-out for youth during the 1920s and 1930s in LaGrange, (currently the home of Red Pepper Deli). In the mornings Margaret Burge, Bonnie Dixon, Lib Walsh, Alma Hess, and Ruth Williamson (with sons Tommy and Jimmy in tow) would meet for coffee. After school, the LaGrange High School crowd gathered around for cokes and dancing. The place was also packed after movies (D.W. Griffith Movie theatre was close by) and ball games. Beer was served for adults back then! Nancy Doty recalls that Mary D's pimento cheese was the best. Peggy Burge submitted Mary D's Pimento Cheese recipe that her mother, Margaret made often (you can use Mary D's Quick Mayonnaise or store bought)

MARY D'S PIMENTO CHEESE

Hand grate a pound of sharp cheddar cheese and combine with a little, finely chopped onion, finely chopped green pepper (2 tablespoons), jar of small pimentos and enough Mayonnaise (Kraft) to hold together well.

QUICK MAYONNAISE

1 egg
½ cup vinegar
1 cup Wesson oil
Juice of one lemon
1 teaspoon salt
1 teaspoon dry mustard
1 teaspoon pepper
1 cup of Eagle Brand condensed milk

Put in a quart jar and shake for five minutes (or blender for 2 minutes). Keep refrigerated.

PEACOCK COTTAGES

Peacock Cottages was built by Maude Peacock Bottorff around 1936 and operated by her until about 1950. This motor court (motel) was located in Goshen, Kentucky on the north side of U.S. Hwy. 42 opposite the TIN-DOR Thoroughbred Horse Farm. By 1972 the several small cottages had been raised and the main building remodeled into a two story front with tall columns. The screened porch at right had previously been enclosed and a fireplace chimney was added at that end. Maude P. Bottorff was the sister of Jessie Peacock Peck.

(Oldham County Historical Society Collection)

Favorite Places to Eat and Visit

SOO'S INN HUNGARIAN RESTAURANT *Submitted by Nancy Theiss*

Steve and Merika Soos were owners of Soo's Hungarian Restaurant during the 1970s and early 1980s in LaGrange, now the location of Mike's Fish House. Steve was trained to cook in the Tatra Mountains of Czechoslovakia and people still remember his wonderful wedding platter and fried fish on Fridays. This recipe is taken from an article about Steve in the Oldham Era, Nov. 3, 1977 when Steve appeared as a guest chef for Shillito's Department Store at Oxmoor Mall in Louisville.

STEVE SOOS VEAL PAPRIKAS

1 pound veal (can be shoulder cut)
3 tablespoons shortening
1 medium diced onion
1 clove minced garlic
1 tablespoon paprika
1½ teaspoon black pepper
1 green diced pepper
1 tomato diced
3 bay leaves
1 tablespoon sour cream
1 cup veal stock, beef stock or water
1 tablespoon cooking flour

Cut meat in 1½ inch pieces and put aside. Melt shortening; add onion, green pepper, and tomato. Cook slowly until vegetables are tender. Add paprika mixed in veal stock or water. Add meat, salt, garlic, pepper, bay leaves. Cover and cook in 325 F degree oven until meat is tender. Take from oven and put on top of stove again. Mix together very well sour cream, flour, and 1 cup of water in a container. Add this to meat mixture- boil all together for 5–7 minutes. Serve with egg dumplings or rice.

SCHOOLHOUSE ANTIQUE MALL LUNCH BOX TEA ROOM *Submitted by Ruth Klingenfus*

Ballardsville Elementary School on the corner of Hwy. 22 and Hwy. 53 became the location of an antique mall that was run by the Klingenfus Family. Ruth shares their recipe for Boiled Dressing that can be used for salads, deviled eggs, or anything else that calls for mayonnaise.

BOILED DRESSING

Mix in skillet
2 cups sugar with 4 eggs
Add to skillet 1 cup vinegar, 1 cup water and 2 tablespoons margarine

Cook on low until thick and then refrigerate.

IRISH ROVER TOO *Submitted by Siobhan and Michael Reidy*

The Reidy's share their story about Irish food traditions and give us their recipe for Grandma Reidy's Brown Soda Bread that is served daily at both their restaurants in LaGrange and on Frankfort Avenue in Louisville.

Many Irish Americans consider Corned Beef and Cabbage to be a typical Irish dish, but, in fact, corned beef is not commonly found in Ireland or at least it wasn't when Michael was growing up in County Clare on Ireland's western coast. If there can be said to be a national dish, it would, without a doubt, be Bacon & Cabbage which is not widely known abroad but is made and consumed in every Irish home on a weekly basis.

Bacon & Cabbage is Michael's favorite meal, and it is what his mother prepared for us on the first night of our first visit to Ireland after our marriage. She made a delicious parsley sauce and accompanied the boiled bacon and cabbage with lots of floury Irish potatoes. It was a memorable meal but, for several reasons, this is not the recipe we're going to share with you.

While easy to make, the ingredients are difficult to procure outside of Ireland. Sure, we can get cabbage and potatoes, but not the way they grow them there. And the real problem is the bacon, which is what the Irish call all pork which is not ham (the leg, also called "gammon"), innards or trotters.

Like American bacon, Irish bacon is cured, but the similarities end there. Back bacon is cured with spices and is cooked as a roast or in chops. "Streaky bacon" with a little more fat on it is fried up for the famous Irish Breakfasts. The brined shoulder or collar of the pig is known as boiling bacon and is the traditional cut for Bacon & Cabbage.

Although a few websites and US butchers can provide bacon and other typically Irish meats, for simplicity's sake, we though it best to provide the recipe for another item that went into that memorable meal, (and every other meal we've ever had in Ireland) Brown Soda Bread.

Until recently, this easy to make homemade bread was a staple in every Irish home, but in recent times busy Irish women have moved away from homebaking. The bread must be eaten within 24 hours, and it is best with high quality butter, such as the European butters sold at specialty stores. It also goes brilliantly with smoked salmon or a smoked fish pate.

Irish Rover Logo (courtesy of Michael and Siobhan Reidy)

GRANDMA REIDY'S BROWN SODA BREAD

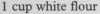

1 cup white flour
2 cups whole wheat flour, preferably coarse
½ teaspoon salt
1 teaspoon baking soda
1 tablespoon butter
1+ cups of buttermilk

Preheat over to 450 F degrees. Stir dry ingredients together with a fork. Cut butter into dry mix.

Make a well in the center and pour in buttermilk. Stir to mix well, making a slightly sticky dough. Turn out onto floured surface. Working the dough as little as possible, pat it into a round loaf. Place on a greased baking sheet and bake for 10 minutes. Lower heat to 375 F degrees and continue baking for 30–40 minutes. Bread is done if tapping the bottom of the loaf produces a hollow sound.

Favorite Places to Eat and Visit

WESTPORT GENERAL STORE

Since the town of Westport was created in 1780 there has always been a Westport General Store except for a period between 1998 and 2003 when the store was closed. Will Crawford and Laura Crawford bought the store building in 2003 and revamped the concept and added a restaurant. Customers can still buy necessities at the store but the real center-piece of the Westport General Store is the upscale southern Cuisine. Guests drive from all around to sample their unique gourmet vittles such as Bison Rib-eye steaks topped with Tobacco Onions, Shrimp wrapped in Country Ham served with stone ground grits and collard greens, and Blackened catfish with dirty rice.

The Westport General Store was the first restaurant in Oldham county with a full bar after alcohol sales were permitted in the county in 2004. Will Crawford uses local ingredients and products whenever possible in order to support the community and the local farmers.

Westport General Store logo (courtesy of Will and Laura Crawford)

WESTPORT GENERAL STORE BISON RIB-EYE WITH GRITS AND GREENS

Greens:

Yields about 6 servings (we just cook until there is enough). Take 2 bunches of collard greens and trim into bite size pieces (no stalk). Rinse in cold water three times, draining the water each time. Heat a pan big enough for the greens. Remember the greens will shrink by half after cooking. Add oil to pan and about 4 pieces of bacon. Cook until medium done. Add the rinsed and trimmed greens along with a thinly sliced onion and one quarter cup of chicken stock. Mix together and cook until shrunk by half. Add salt and pepper to taste, half a jalapenos pepper, and sprinkle crushed red pepper. Cook until tender.

Grits:

Bring 4½ cups of water to a boil. Stir in 1 cup of Weisenberger yellow grits. (These are the best stone ground grits on the market) Reduce heat and simmer for 20–25 minutes, stirring occasionally, cover and simmer until done. Add salt and cream or half and half to taste.

Bison Rib-eye:

We use Kentucky Bison Company meat. It is raised a few miles from our restaurant and this makes the meat taste even better, as anyone knows home grown is the best. At home I marinate the meat in a half Worcestershire and half soy sauce mix. In the winter I grill the meat inside in the fireplace. Nothing better!

Have your steaks cut into 8oz portions. Grill to desired temperature. Medium rare to medium is best. Remember Bison meat is lean and over cooking can make it tough. Thinly slice a red onion and toss in seasoned flour. Deep fry till golden brown. Serve on top of steak.

Women's Lunch at Westport Schoolhouse (reprint permission of Courier-Journal, November 5, 1960)

Famous People

This chapter highlights a few "famous" folks who have lived or visited here.

D. W. GRIFFITH

Reprinted with permission by Joseph Woodson Oglesby from his book Dinner with D. W. Griffith and Other Memories

Whenever Cousin David (film director David Wark Griffith) returned home to LaGrange, he was a regular diner at Grandmother's Sunday dinners. One memorable Sunday, Granddaddy answered the door-something he rarely did-with the news that Cousin David had arrived from New York the day before and was expected home anytime. Grandmother had been in the kitchen since dawn preparing his favorite dishes. He especially loved her high-rising biscuits and lemon meringue pie. Glassware and china sparkled on the long dining room table. Even Granddaddy had been polished. He wore a black suit and black string tie and had been given specific instruction by my grandmother not to stuff his napkin into his collar but to lay it across his lap.

Cousin David wouldn't have cared how Granddaddy used his napkin. He and granddaddy had grown up together, double first cousins who were as close as brothers. Granddaddy used to tease Cousin David about his prominent nose saying it would provide plenty of shade on a sunny summer's day. Cousin David teased him back, calling my hefty grandfather "a delicate-looking little thing." Granddaddy had supplied Cousin David with country clothes and boots as a costume for his first acting part, a role in a church play in Louisville.

Taken from D. W. Griffith Production, "Broken Blossom", (Oldham County Historical Society Collection)

Other relatives began to arrive and finally Cousin David. He was still a handsome man with a commanding voice like that of his father, Colonel Jacob Wark "Roaring Jake" Griffith, who led the Confederate cavalry charges during the Civil War. It was near Christmas, and Cousin David had brought presents for everyone. His chauffeur, Richard Reynolds, brought them in, wrapped in boxes with large bows in two large shopping bags.

Sitting in Granddaddy's easy chair, his face reddened by the fire blazing in the potbellied stove, Cousin David called out names and presented the gifts, all bought at fashionable New York stores. He presented my Aunt Evelyn, perhaps his favorite young cousin, with a silver bracelet from Tiffany's. He had wanted to take her to Hollywood many years before, seeing her as another Mary Pickford, "America's Sweetheart." But my grandmother had refused to allow it. He also wrote checks to everyone, my granddaddy and daddy and uncles each receiving one hundred dollars.

Grandmother then announced dinner, and everyone sat down at the long dining table. Halfway through the meal, Cousin David told everyone he planned to marry a young actress named Evelyn Baldwin, who had appeared in his last film, "The Struggle." He said they would be married as soon as his divorce from Linda Arvidson Griffith was granted. The newlyweds planned to live in LaGrange for a while as he worked on his autobiography.

Oldham County native, D. W. Griffith, has been called the father of the modern film industry. He was the first to develop epic films, with large sets and themes that often ran over 2 hours, compared to previously produced film clips of less than 10 minutes. (Oldham County Historical Society Collection)

"That'll give me a chance to whip you at the pool table," my grandfather quipped.

The dinner was going beautifully, with Cousin David thoroughly enjoying the meal and complimenting my grandmother on her cooking, until the conversation turned to movies.

"I think you are helping the Devil with his work," Grandmother said suddenly, staring at Cousin David.

"I'm sorry you feel that way Jenny, but I believe my movies are a force for good."

"I can't see how a parade of naked women can improve anyone's morals," Grandmother said.

He managed a faint smile and answered evenly. "I'm afraid you have a narrow view, Jenny."

Cousin David was right, of course, about Grandmother's having a narrow view. She was a religious fanatic. That was her only fault. Even the most common pleasures-drinking and dancing and smoking-were scarlet sins to her way of thinking. Any woman who smoked was a harlot. Any man who took a drink of hard liquor was a Satan's disciple.

Her fanaticism took some strange paths. Sometimes, before the entire congregation of DeHaven Memorial Baptist Church, she would rattle the family skeletons and asked the congregation to pray for the sinners. In a dark purple dress, her gray hair pulled back severely from her face and wound into a hard bun, she'd clear her throat and start. Her eldest son, Joseph, drank to excess. Her second daughter, Ruth, had married a Catholic! Her words rang out with suffocating force, drowning even the whoosh of the palm shaped fans on a hot summer day. The words became a torrent, madly swirling; but just as quickly the torrent stopped, and she sat down, calmly fanning herself.

Somehow her zealotry never troubled my grandfather. He would either ignore her ranting and raving, or start playing and singing when she began to sermonize.

God rest her soul. She was the best cook in Oldham County.

GRANDMOTHER'S LEMON MERINGUE PIE

Pie Crust
    3 cups premium flour
    ½ level teaspoon baking powder
    1 level teaspoon salt
    ¾ cup lard

Sift together dry ingredients, add a pinch of sugar, and work in lard with knife; then moisten with water. Place dough on a board dusted with flour and roll flat, and then put in pie pan. Trim edge and punch holes in bottom and sides to keep it from rising. Bake until done (350F degrees about 15 minutes). Allow to cool.

Lemon Filling
    ¾ cup sugar
    ¾ cup boiling water
    1 tablespoon flour
    2 egg yolks
    3 tablespoons lemon juice
    1 teaspoon butter
    Grated rind of one lemon

Mix flour and sugar, adding boiling water constantly. Cook two minutes before adding butter, egg yolks, rind and juice. Pout into piecrust and add meringue. Return to oven and bake until meringue is tinged a soft brown.

Meringue
    2 egg whites
    1 teaspoon water
    2 tablespoons powdered sugar
    1 teaspoon lemon juice or ¼ teaspoon vanilla extract

Beat egg whites until stiff. Gradually add powdered sugar. Continue whipping and add lemon juice or vanilla extract.

ANNIE FELLOWS JOHNSTON AND *THE LITTLE COLONEL*
Recipe and excerpt from Louise Marker

In the early 1900's, Pewee Valley was home to Annie Fellows Johnston while she was writing The Little Colonel books, a popular series among the young girls of that day. The fictitious setting of Lloydsburg was inspired by Pewee Valley and the characters were often based on actual townspeople. The main character, Lloyd, is a pert little girl of about 5 years when the series opens. Because she can be just as stubborn as her grandfather, The Colonel, she is called the Little Colonel. There was a movie starring Shirley Temple as Lloyd and Lionel Barrymore as her grandfather depicting the initial book *The Little Colonel*. The following except is taken from that book while Lloyd is visiting her grandfather at his home, The Locust.

"So you did come to see grandpa after all," he cried triumphantly. "Come here and give me a kiss. Seems to me you've been staying away a mighty long time."

As she stood beside him with his arm around her, Walker came in with a tray full of dishes.

"We're going to have a regular little tea-party," said the Colonel.

Lloyd watched with sparkling eyes as Walker set out the rare old-fashioned dishes. There was a fat little silver sugar-bowl with a butterfly perched on each side to form the handles and there was a slim, graceful cream-pitcher shaped like a lily.

"They belonged to your great-great-grandmother," said the Colonel, "and they're going to be yours some day if you grow up and have a house of your own."

The expression on her beaming face was worth a fortune to the Colonel.

When Walker pushed her chair up to the table, she turned to her grandfather with shining eyes.

"Oh, it's just like a pink story," she cried, clapping her hands. "The shades on the can'les, the icin' on the cake, and' the posies in the bowl,—why even the jelly is that colah too. Oh, my darlin' little teacup! It's jus' like a pink rosebud. I'm so glad I came!"

This is the nicest pahty I evah was at," remarked the Little Colonel, as Walker helped her to jam the third time. Her grandfather chuckled.

One Saturday, Mom Beck, the famous and faithful cook, took a picnic basket for the little colonel and her friends. As the Little Colonel spied the basket, she cried with joy, "What have you in the basket?"

The cook replied, "Honey chil, I have some of Mrs. Joy's jelly cookies.

Book Jacket cover taken from first editions of The Land of the Little Colonel by Annie Fellows Johnston written about life in Pewee Valley (Oldham County Historical Society collection).

MRS. JOY'S JELLY COOKIES

1 cup sugar
1 cup butter
3 egg whites
2 cups flour
2 teaspoons baking powder
¾ cup sweet milk

Drop cookie batter by teaspoonful on greased baking sheet. Bake at 350 degrees. When cookies are done and still warm, spread small amount of favorite jelly on one cookie and place other cookie on top to make a sandwich.

Sprinkle with powdered sugar while warm.

Queen's Luncheon

Reprinted with permission from Louisville Magazine, July 1986 written by Lillian Marshall

We can't know the innermost feeling of Queen Elizabeth II on a day this May when her party, headquartered at Lane's End Farm in Woodford County, took an unpublicized side trip to visit Warner and Harriet Jones' Hermitage Farm in Oldham County and enjoy an informal luncheon. Still, while only a few were privileged to lunch with the Queen, all of us can share the menu and a splendid recipe for one of the courses designed and prepared by a local English expatriate engaged by Mr. Jones to help with the royal affair.

She is Yvonne Williams, who styles herself a horsewoman, gardener, painter and cook, in that order. A tall brunette, attractive and sparely built as befits a person who loves the outdoors, she rejects the title of caterer.

"I do enjoy cooking, but it is a small part of my life. I have had no formal training. And I certainly don't work up menus for myself. In summer I live out of my garden on salad and greens."

But her superior cooking is a talent not easily hidden; she invariably gets called upon to "help out friends when they're entertaining."

The Good Queen Beckons.
"Mrs. Jones called last Christmas day about the luncheon date," Williams remembers. "At the time she didn't know the Queen herself was coming. She was expecting the trainer and his wife. So I said fine. Later, when we found out Her Majesty was coming, I began to be excited and nervous."

Everyone concerned was sworn to secrecy. How can you be excited and nervous in secret?

"Not so easily," Williams says.

"The Queen made her own selection from the three menus we presented. Oh yes, she really does decide for herself. We offered a luncheon based on tenderloin of beef, one on creamed mushrooms and sausage and one on chicken."

Now, one wonders, wouldn't a queen pick and choose things from every menu, each so carefully planned as an entity? Perhaps the soup from Menu I, and the entrée from Menu II, dessert from the third?

"Oh no, she chose the chicken menu exactly as it was given."

Here's the menu chosen by the Queen, prepared by Yvonne Williams and served by two waiters to the 12 people, royal and otherwise, gathered at the Jones' table.

> Cold Curried Eggplant Soup
> Chicken Stroganov
> Wild rice
> Fresh Asparagus
> Bibb Lettuce and Watercress lightly dressed in
>   Oil and Vinegar
> Home-made rolls
> Cold Lemon Soufflé and Fresh Sliced
> Strawberries

Stalking Fresh. Some cooks talk fresh ingredients; Williams does some thing about freshness. She stalks it. The miles don't count when she makes the rounds of her favorite purveyors.

She favors Paul's Market in St. Matthews "Because they went out of their way to find watercress and perfect strawberries." Her asparagus comes from Pin Oak Farm in Lexington, her mushrooms from Bluegrass Mushroom Farm in Middletown, and for her meats, she finds Paul Fischer, also in Middletown, quite reliable.

That's a lot of running around," She admits, "But it's worth it to get the best. If you are going to spend the time cooking, you might as well use the best ingredients."

Yvonne Williams is an accidental Kentuckian, born on a farm in Sussex in the south of England. "We had horses and ponies; I was hunting by the time I was four." She recalls. In 1967, she came to the States for a short

Queen Elizabeth with Warner Jones at Hermitage Farm, 1986 (Oldham County Historical Society Collection).

visit and never left. "Kentucky was a mistake! I came here and bought two horses. They were too big to fit in the car, so I had to stay. Now I try to get back to England every year or year-and-a-half to visit my mother, brothers and sisters.

Clean Plants and a Clean Plate. Williams does her gardening in raised beds situated between the barn that houses a dozen Thoroughbred yearlings in her care and her own tidy house, near Brownsboro in Oldham County. Threatening to uproot lettuce that would put the supermarket's puny greens to shame, she munches on sweet pea pods from plants still in flower and observes her perfect broccoli with satisfaction.

"I don't use anything on these plants," she says with her still-discernible British accent. "No bug spray, no fertilizer."

Her spinach crop is ready to be transferred from garden to freezer, her zucchini about to come on strong.

Lovely chives, she notes. Lovely, too, the Bibb she'd planted at the regular time, hoping it would be ready for the Queen's visit (and it was).

She casts her eye on the too-late parsley bed: "I had to get parsley from a neighbor, for the Queen's lunch because it wasn't ready!"

The woman who moves so easily from the yearling barn to the gourmet kitchen gives the impression that she doesn't have to find things to occupy her; they find her. Still to do this day was a dessert for a friend who had dinner guests coming, then up before sunrise for The Three Day Event at the Kentucky Horse Park near Lexington. She and a friend were doing the scales, weighing riders and tack before and after the cross country section.

A quick last question: Did Her Majesty enjoy the luncheon?

"She cleaned her plate"

A Royal Soup

This soup, taken from the Williams menu, has been taste tested by HRH Queen Elizabeth of England.

Cold Curried Eggplant Soup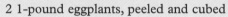

2 1-pound eggplants, peeled and cubed
1½ tablespoons salt
2 small onions, finely chopped
2 garlic cloves, minced
2 tablespoons olive oil
1 tablespoon curry powder
2 quarts fresh chicken broth
½ cup chopped fresh parsley, divided
1 – 2 tablespoons fresh lemon juice
Salt and pepper to taste

Combine eggplant cubes with salt in colander. Allow to stand 30 minutes. Rinse thoroughly under cold water, drain and press out all possible excess water.

Heat oil in heavy four-quart saucepan, and add onion and garlic; stir over moderate heat until

onion is transparent. Add curry powder and continue cooking and stirring for another minute. Add broth and bring to boiling. Add eggplant, reduce heat and simmer, covered for ½ hour.

Using blender or food processor, puree soup mixture in batches adding half the chopped parsley during the process. Then pass soup through a food mill or strainer into a bowl, season to taste with salt and pepper. Cool soup, then chill at least 4 hours (preferably overnight). Just before serving, stir in lemon juice and sprinkle remaining parsley over the top; taste and correct seasonings. Serves 8–12.

Note: chilling has the effect of lowering the flavor of seasoning, always correct the seasoning when soup is cold.

KATE MATTHEWS

Miss Kate Matthews, a noted photographer from Pewee Valley, had work featured in "Photography in America" a major exhibition of the best American photography at the Whitney Museum of American Art. Approximately 100 examples of her work are now part of the permanent collection of the University of Louisville Photographic Archives. Her family home which has since burned, was located at the corner of Ash Avenue and LaGrange Road and was named Clovercroft. The following is a vignette description of their typical Christmas celebration. It was published in the December 1975 edition of the "The Call of the Pewee", Pewee Valley's monthly publication.

VIGNETTES OF PEWEE VALLEY BY FLORENCE DICKERSON

Christmas at Clovercroft

Christmas at "Clovercroft," the Matthews' spacious home, was always a very exciting and festive time of year. Weeks before the day there was an air of secrecy and much went on behind closed doors for everyone was making gifts. No one would even give a hint so that the recipient of each gift could be completely surprised.

Although the Matthews usually did not have a Christmas tree, the house was carefully decorated. Hemlock and holly were cut from trees on the property and Kate, the photographer, would drive her pony cart into the woods and gather cedar. By the day before Christmas all the pictures, sconces and fireplace mantels were framed with evergreen boughs. The stairway to the second floor was twined with garlands of greens and even the gateposts had their holiday decorations.

Christmas eve the Matthews would go caroling at the houses of all their friends. Each year they and the neighbors stopped at Mr. Frank Gatchel's to hear him read Dicken's "Christmas Carol."

The night before Christmas, whenever an adult awakened from his sleep, he jingled sleigh bells. This was to the delight of the children because they believed it to be Santa Claus going about visiting the homes in Pewee.

The year that Aunt Jay (Jessie Joy Matthews) returned from Berlin was the most exciting Christmas. She had been abroad studying piano with Thedor Leschetizky, the renowned teacher. When the doors to the parlor were opened, there was a magnificent grand piano, a gift from her father.

Another year the husband of one of the granddaughters who lived in the East brought a radio. No one was to know about it until Christmas morning, so in the middle of the night he managed to open one of the parlor windows and put this marvel of the age on a table amid holly and hemlock decorations. Everyone was ecstatic when the radio, one of the first in the community, was revealed.

When Grandfather Matthews (Lucian Jex) was unable to plan any unusual gifts he would give everyone a gold coin. A marble top table was draped with velvet and the coins arranged on this. Grandmother Matthews always received the largest gold piece and the others received one of less value down to the youngest member of the family who was given the smallest.

Before the day of pre-tied bows and rolls of Christmas paper, gifts were wrapped in original designs. The gifts, too, were original endeavors, beautiful handmade creations, embroidery, or paintings. Kate very often gave a photograph; one that was especially apropos. The gifts were not opened until Christmas morning and then there was much ceremony. It was a tradition that if you were to say "Christmas gift" to anyone, they were to give you a gift, although you were not required to give them one. Since much thought and preparation had been made for this occasion, no one was overlooked and there was a gift for everyone. The poems that accompanied the handmade remembrances were as cherished as the gift, and these were read aloud before the gift was opened.

Often during the holidays friends gathered in the parlor to hear the Matthews' music and to sing the Christmas songs they all liked so much. Jay played the piano or organ; Florence, the piano; Edwin, the violin and Kate, the violin. Tis said that Kate never played the violin very well and some would sing a bit "off key," but all joined heartily. When it was no longer appropriate to sing Christmas carols, there were thoughts of the next Christmas.

A Clovercroft Christmas Dinner Menu
Serves 8

Cornish Hens
Wild Rice Stuffing
Artichokes and Mushrooms
Cranberry Port Mold
Individual Plum Cake Flambé
Hot Rolls
Coffee
Well Chilled Chablis

Artichokes and Mushrooms

2 15-oz cans artichoke hearts, drained
1 quart package fresh mushrooms
4 tablespoons butter
1½ teaspoon salt
2 tablespoons lemon juice
1 tablespoon minced onion
1 cup fine bread crumbs browned
    in 2 tablespoons butter

Cook mushrooms and onion in the 4 tablespoons butter until tender. Arrange this in a greased baking dish. Drizzle with salt and drizzle lemon juice over all. Sprinkle browned crumbs on top of the vegetables. Bake in a 350 degree oven for 20 minutes.

Cornish Hens

1 large hen per person
1 lemon
¼ cup butter
1 teaspoon thyme
1 tablespoon salt

Wash and dry hens thoroughly. Salt the birds inside and out. Cut lemon into 8 slices. Using 1 slice of lemon per hen, rub each one inside and out. Mix thyme and butter. Set this mixture aside to be dotted over the top of each bird after it is stuffed.

Wild Rice Stuffing

1 package wild rice—prepared according to
    directions on the box
¼ cup butter
¼ cup chopped onions
¾ teaspoon salt
¾ teaspoon thyme
¾ teaspoon marjoram
½ cup slivered toasted almonds, pistachio nuts
    or raisins

Sauté onions in butter. Mix rice and nuts. Season with salt, thyme and marjoram. Stuff hens with this mixture, dot each bird with reserved butter-thyme mixture. Bake uncovered 1–1½ hours at 325 degrees, basting hens with pan juices 2–3 times.

Famous People

CRANBERRY PORT MOLD

2 3-oz packages raspberry jello
16-oz can whole cranberry sauce
8¾-oz can undrained crushed pineapple
¾ cup Port wine
¼ cup chopped walnuts

Dissolve gelatin in 2 cups boiling water. Stir in cranberry sauce, pineapple and wine. Chill till partially set. Fold in nuts. Pour mixture into a 6½ cup mold or 10–12 individual molds.

PLUM CAKE FLAMBÉ

1 cup Crisco oil
2 cups sugar
3 eggs
2 cups self-rising flour
1 teaspoon cinnamon
1 teaspoon ground cloves
2 small baby food jars of plums
1 cup chopped pecans
1 or 2 teaspoons red food coloring

Cream oil, sugar and eggs. Then add flour and dry ingredients. Fold in plums and nuts. Bake in a greased and floured tube pan for 50 minutes at 350 degrees. Sprinkle with 4X sugar.

To make individual petite cakes spoon the batter into well-greased paper hot-drink cups. Bake for about 30–35 minutes. Cool a few minutes then turn out of cups. Drizzle with about a teaspoon of rum when ready to inflame. This is a moist cake and will keep in the refrigerator for some time.

Organizations

Oldham County's civic pride rests with the talents and energy of the clubs, churches and organizations that tirelessly contribute to our community. We are grateful to the following for sharing their recipes and stories about their history and food culture.

Front cover of the LaGrange Cookbook circa 1925 (Oldham County Historical Society collection).

CRESTWOOD CIVIC CLUB

The following foreword appeared in the Second addition of the Crestwood Community Cookbook published by the Crestwood Civic Club in 1973.

The Crestwood Civic Club was formed on November 20, 1914. The original purpose of civic betterment through civic pride has been fulfilled in various ways by the officers and members who have contributed greatly of their time and effort through the years.

Almost immediately the Club entered into the first of their projects—raising money to help work on the roads. And so it has continued; however, space does not permit us to list all their achievements.

In 1917 they put the first warning bell at the L&N crossing; in 1918 they helped pay for installing lights in the school; in 1920 helped build the walk to the school. We really helped brighten up the town in 1927 by installing the street lights which we still maintain today.

To help pay for the new club house built in 1952 the ladies became active in many money making projects—serving suppers, Sunday meals, birthday calendar and bazaars to name only a few.

Service to the community is foremost in our efforts today as shown through our annual scholarship and beautification program. Our chief source of income comes from our annual bazaar held each November and wedding reception catering.

The goal and enthusiasm for civic betterment is a priceless heritage from the members who have gone before. May we always be worthy of it.

Table Setting and Serving— These guidelines originally appeared in the first edition of the Crestwood Community Cookbook published in 1930 and were also included in the second edition.

Tablecloths should be laid without wrinkles and perfectly straight.

The sharp edge of knives should be turned toward the plate.

Bowls of spoons and tines of forks must be turned up.

Place the knives and spoons at the right of the plate in order used, beginning at the extreme right.

Place the butter plate and tumbler at the right of the plate.

Place the napkin at the left with the open edge at the edge of the table.

If the bread and butter plate is used place it at the left.

Bread must be freshly cut.

Water glass must be kept filled and should not be lifted from the table in being filled.

Everything used for one course must be removed first, then remove the soiled dishes and lastly the clean dishes.

Remove from right when possible but never reach in front of anyone.

Always go to the left when a person is to take anything from the tray.

Always go to the right when you are to place anything on the table.

Remove crumbs before the dessert is served.

BUTTERMILK BISCUITS

This recipe was submitted to the Crestwood Community Cook Book by Mrs. M. C. Stoess

2 cups sifted flour
½ teaspoon salt
3 teaspoons baking powder
½ teaspoon soda
3 tablespoons butter or margarine
¾ cup butter milk

Sift flour, baking powder and soda together. Blend in margarine and add buttermilk kneading lightly. Roll to ¾" thickness and cut with small cutter. Dab top with melted margarine and able 450 F degrees for 12 minutes.

LITTLE COLONEL PLAYHOUSE *Submitted by Patti Nuremburger*

The Little Colonel Playhouse in Pewee Valley is the oldest continuously operating community theatre in Kentucky. Chartered in 1957, the players will celebrate their 50th anniversary during the 2006–2007 season. They've come a long way from their annual presentation of three one-act plays to the current 2005–2006 season featuring 5 plays, a youth production and a children's workshop presentation. It is one of the few theaters today that is completely autonomous, self-supporting and operated by all-volunteer board members, directors, actors, actresses and backstage crews.

During intermission of each play, the audience is invited to the Green Room to mingle and enjoy refreshments. The traditional punch (which has been served at every performance for most of the last thirty years) is a refreshing and pretty mixture of half parts cranberry juice and ginger ale. The Hospitality servers pour it over ice just before the lights go on for intermission.

A popular night at the theater is the opening night of each play which features a delicious candlelight dinner complete with wine and dessert. In the early days, the dinner was prepared and served by volunteer members. Later, dinners were prepared by women in the Pewee Valley Presbyterian church as a fund-raiser for their projects. For the last several years, dinners have been prepared by the Pewee Valley Women's Club, as a fund-raiser for their projects. The dinners are delicious and varied. The most recent menu was:

The Little Colonel Players

Little Colonel Playhouse Logo (courtesy of Patti Nuermberger).

Green salad with balsamic vinaigrette
Chicken Alfredo with pasta
Hot bread with butter
Sweet Repast
Wine, water and coffee

SWEET REPAST

This recipe is from "The Valley Bountiful", a cookbook published by the Pewee Valley Women's Club.

First layer:
   1 cup chopped pecans
   1 ½ cup flour
   1 ¼ sticks margarine (room temperature)

Second layer:
   1 8-oz package cream cheese
   1 cup powdered sugar
   1 cup Cool Whip

Third Layer:
   2 small boxes any flavor instant pudding
   3 cups cold milk

Fourth layer:
   1 cup Cool Whip
   Nuts (top with)

First layer: Cream margarine, then add rest of ingredients. Mix well and press into 9 x 12 inch pan. Bake 25 minutes at 350 degrees. Cool. Second layer: Cream ingredients together and spread over top pf baked first layer. Third layer: Mix and add to top of second layer. Fourth layer: Spread on top of third layer and top with nuts.

OLDHAM COUNTY BOOSTERS *Submitted by Steve Greenwell*

The Oldham County Boosters needed more money to fund their projects. At the time I was a member of the Falls City Pork Producers who had a great recipe they had "stolen" from the Iowa Pork Producers. Using their recipe I got out my grill and showed the Oldham County Boosters how to cook pork chops, and they were off.

Since then the Falls City Pork Producers have quit raising hogs or grown too old and tired to cook but still have enough money to fund an annual scholarship. The Oldham County Boosters, however, still continue to grill the pork chops at football games.

KENTUCKY STYLE BARBEQUED PORK CHOPS

6 pork ribs or loin chops cut 1" to 1¼" thick
2½ cups water
1 tablespoon sugar
1 tablespoon black pepper
2 tablespoons cooking oil
¼ cup vinegar
1 tablespoon salt
¼ cup chopped onion
1 garlic clove, minced
1 teaspoon red pepper
2 teaspoons chili powder
1 teaspoon red pepper sauce
1 teaspoon dry mustard
3 tablespoons Worcestershire sauce

Combine all ingredients except pork chops in a 1 quart sauce pan and bring to a boil. Reduce heat and simmer for 5 minutes. Barbeque sauce is better if allowed to stand in refrigerator overnight to blend flavors. Warm sauce before using.

~ops on grill over low coals. (Coals should be ash gray). Grill for 12–15 minutes on each side,
~rushing frequently with BBQ sauce.

Mount Tabor Fish Fry *Submitted by Al Klingenfus*

The fish fry has been the main money maker for the Mount Tabor United Methodist Men since the new church building was completed in 1977–78. It began as a once-a-year dinner and for $4.50 you were served fish, baked beans, slaw, fried potatoes and bread. This year the men plan 5 fish fries and offer both dine-in for $8 and carry out for $7. The money raised is used to fund various church projects ranging from flowers to septic systems.

FRIED FISH

60 pounds codfish
2 5-pound bags yellow or white corn meal
2½ pound flour
Salt and pepper to taste

Dredge fish in cornmeal mixture and drop in deep-fat fryer filled with vegetable oil or corn oil heated to 350 degrees. Fish is done when it floats to the top.

Two or three times a year, the men use Charlie Brown's recipe for beer batter in addition to the regular corn meal mix.

CHARLIE BROWN'S BEER BATTER

6 dozen eggs
8 beers

Mix beer and eggs well then dip fish and then roll in the corn meal mixture and fry as usual.

CHARLIE BROWN'S FRIED POTATOES

Potatoes
Garlic powder
Salt and pepper

Parboil the potatoes until fork tender. Quarter or cut into steak fry size. Place a layer of potatoes in a large pan. Sprinkle with garlic powder, salt and pepper and add more potato layers. In batches, place in the deep-fat fryer. Potatoes are done when they float.

DON TAYLOR'S COLE SLAW

Pre-mixed cabbage (slaw mix)

4 quarts of salad dressing
2 cups sugar
2 cups cider vinegar
Salt and pepper to taste "less than a cup and more than a teaspoon" —Don Taylor
Makes 1½ gallons of dressing

Mix cabbage and dressing together and chill until ready to serve.

DON TAYLOR'S TARTAR SAUCE

2 quarts salad dressing
1 pint sweet relish
1 cup minced onion

Mix ingredients and chill.

DON TAYLOR'S BAKED BEANS

1½ cup brown sugar
1 cup molasses
2 cups onions
3 gallons pork-n-beans

~ther and cook.

PEWEE VALLEY WOMEN'S CLUB

Submitted by Patti Nuremburger

In the 1970's and 1980's, the Pewee Valley Women's Club hosted an annual fall bazaar to raise funds for their community projects which included college scholarships, children's art competitions and a preschool. The club women worked for months making crafts, sewing, knitting, cooking, canning and preserving items to be sold. The Bazaar began at 10am and shopping continued till a sit-down luncheon was served. By 2pm tidying up began, money was counted and then the women went home to rest their feet!

Pewee Valley Women's Club Meeting Building (courtesy of Patti Nuermberger).

There is still a lot of cooking going on in the Pewee Valley Women's Club. Each monthly meeting begins at 10am and concludes with a delicious lunch. The Club also has Gourmet Group evening meals several times a year that also include the husbands.

The Bazaar luncheon menu varied from year to year, but a favorite one was printed in the cookbook that the Pewee Valley Women's Club published in 1985

BAZAAR LUNCHEON MENU

HOT CHICKEN SALAD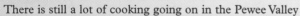

3 cups cooked chicken cubed
1½ cup chopped celery
¾ cup slivered almonds
1 6-oz can water chestnuts, drained and sliced
½ teaspoon salt
2 teaspoons grated onion
3 tablespoons lemon juice
1 can cream of chicken soup
1 cup mayonnaise

Combine and place in greased 9 x 13 casserole dish and top with ¾ cup shredded cheddar cheese and 1½ cup crushed potato chips. Bake at 325 for 45 minutes.

PRETZEL SALAD

2 cups crushed pretzels
¼ cup sugar, divided
½ stick of butter
8-oz package of cream cheese
2 cups Cool Whip
6-oz package strawberry gelatin
2 cups hot pineapple juice
20-oz package frozen strawberries with juice

Soften cream cheese and thaw berries. Add crushed pretzels and ¾ cup sugar to melted butter and spread mixture in 9 x 13 pan that has been greased with oil. Bake at 350 degrees for 10 minutes. Let cool. Heat pineapple juice and dissolve gelatin in it. Add the berries ar Allow to partially set in refrigerator cheese, 1 cup sugar and Cool W. spread over cooled pretzel layer. S set gelatin mixture on top of that an until firm.

Layer Salad

Layer a torn head of lettuce, ½ cup chopped green pepper, ½ cup diced red Bermuda onion, ½ cup chopped celery and 1 small package frozen peas in a 9 x 13 dish. Cover with 1 pint mayonnaise and sprinkle with 2 teaspoons sugar. Crumble 8 slices cooked bacon and ¼ lb shredded cheddar cheese on top. Cover and refrigerate overnight. Do NOT toss before serving.

Blueberry Muffins with topping

½ cup butter
1 cup sugar
2 eggs
1 cup milk
2 cups flour
2 teaspoons baking powder
½ teaspoon salt
1 cup blueberries

Cream together butter, sugar, and eggs. Add dry ingredients alternating with milk. Pour into greased muffin tins.

Topping
2 tablespoons flour
¼ cup sugar
3 teaspoons cinnamon
2 tablespoons melted butter

Mix well with a fork and sprinkle topping over muffins and bake at 400 degrees for 15 minutes.

Chess Pie

1 unbaked pie crust
3 large eggs
1 teaspoon vanilla
1 tablespoon vinegar
1½ cup white sugar
½ stick butter, melted
1 tablespoon yellow corn meal

Beat ingredients at medium speed until mixed. Pour into pie crust. Bake at 400 degrees for 10 minutes then lower temperature to 350 and bake an additional 30 minutes.

**ANOTHER FAVORITE BAZAAR
LUNCHEON MENU INCLUDED:**

Turkey salad
Spinach salad
Benedictine sandwiches
Chocolate-caramel squares

TURKEY SALAD

14 lb turkey cooked and cubed
2 good handfuls grapes
1 lb pecans

4 cups chopped celery
Enough salad dressing to hold salad together
Salt and pepper to taste

CHOCOLATE CARAMEL SQUARES

14 oz bag caramels
⅔ cup evaporated milk, divided
18½ oz package German chocolate cake mix
¾ cup butter, softened
1 cup chopped pecans
6 oz package chocolate chips

Combine caramels and ⅓ cup evaporated milk in top of double boiler, cook and stir till caramels are melted. Remove from heat. Combine cake mix, ⅓ cup milk, butter and mix till dough holds together. Stir in nuts. Press half of cake mixture into greased 9 x 13 pan. Bake 350 degrees for 6 minutes. Sprinkle chocolate chips over crust. Pour caramel mixture over chips, spreading evenly. Crumble remaining cake mixture over the caramel mixture. Return pan to oven and bake 15–18 minutes. Let cool and chill for 30 minutes. Cut into small bars. Yields 5 dozen.

For their fall fundraiser the past several years, the Pewee Valley Woman's Club has hosted a large Arts and Crafts show. This is an all-day event showcasing over 50 exhibitors and artists, baked goods, preserves and featuring the lunch-time favorite: Cowboy Soup.

COWBOY SOUP

Combine in a large soup pan:
    1 small onion chopped and cooked in oil till softened
    1 lb ground beef browned with onion

Drain grease and then add:
    10 oz can diced tomatoes with green chilies
    15 oz can stewed tomatoes
    15 oz can cream style corn
    15 oz can Spanish rice. Note: if you cannot find the can of Spanish rice the dry mix works fine. Be sure to cook the rice according to package directions before adding to the other soup ingredients.

Heat through and serve. Makes about 8 servings

A COLLECT FOR PEWEE VALLEY CLUB WOMEN

Keep us, Oh God, from pettiness;
Let us be large in thought, in word, in deed

Let us be done with fault-finding, and leave off self-seeking.

May we put away pretense and meet each other face to face without self-pity and without prejudice.

May we never be hasty in judgment and always generous.

Let us take time for things; make us to grow calm, serene, and gentle.

Teach us to put into action our better impulses, straight-forward, and unafraid.

Grant that we may realize it is the little things that create differences, that in the big things of life we are as one.

And may we strive to touch and to know the great, common human heart of us all, and, Oh Lord God, let us not forget to be kind!

Index by Food Type

Index